WHAT CHRISTIANS DO

What Christians Do

Living Like Jesus in a Divided World

What Christians Do
978-1-7910-4273-8
978-1-7910-4274-5 *eBook*

What Christians Do DVD
978-1-7910-4277-6

Cover description: The cover presents the title, *What Christians Do*, in large blue and white lettering over an expressive mixed-media background. A dark cross stands at the center, surrounded by abstract brushstrokes in cream, gold, teal, and muted red. Silhouetted figures gathered at the base of the cross suggest a diverse community of people. The subtitle, *Living Like Jesus in a Divided World*, appears in light gold text near the bottom right, while the author's name, Mark Reynolds, is displayed across the top in red. The overall design conveys themes of Christian faith, community, and living faithfully amid division.

MARK REYNOLDS

WHAT CHRISTIANS DO

Living Like Jesus in a Divided World

ABINGDON PRESS | NASHVILLE

What Christians Do

Living Like Jesus in a Divided World

Library of Congress Control Number: 2026945130

978-1-7910-4273-8

MANUFACTURED IN THE UNITED STATES OF AMERICA

CONTENTS

Acknowledgments vii

Introduction: Beyond Belief—Practicing the Way of Jesus . . . ix

1. Christians Practice Surrender 1

2. Christians Practice Forgiveness 17

3. Christians Practice Empathy 39

4. Christians Practice Mercy and Justice 55

5. Christians Wrestle with God 73

6. Christians Share Faith 91

Conclusion: The Work of Grace and the Way of Love 113

Notes 124

WATCH YOUR STUDY ANYTIME, ANYWHERE.

Access your *What Christians Do* videos and leader resources on any device with your Amplify Media account.

GET STARTED IN TWO STEPS

1. Scan the QR code or go to My.AmplifyMedia.com /amplify/redeem

2. Create your free account and enter your companion code

COMPANION CODE
MRED5EH8

ONCE YOU'RE IN

- Videos and leader resources saved to your account
- Watch anytime on phone, tablet, or TV
- Come back anytime at My.AmplifyMedia.com

KEEP TRACK OF YOUR LOG IN INFO

Email ______________________________

Password ______________________________

Companion code subject to expiration. Code may be redeemed only by the recipient of this book. Code may not be transferred or sold separately. Internet connection required.

AMPLIFY™ MEDIA

ACKNOWLEDGMENTS

I am deeply grateful to Sharon Jones, whose insight and encouragement helped me confront self-defeating thoughts and find the courage to write. I am also thankful to Aaron Simmons for his thoughtful feedback on the proposal and early chapters and for believing in this project from the beginning.

Special appreciation goes to Jim Harnish, Justin Holcomb, and Charley Reeb for their guidance and encouragement along the way. To the members of First United Methodist Church of Cocoa Beach, who served as readers during the writing process—your thoughtful reflections and steadfast support reminded me why this work matters.

I am especially thankful for my children—Jobe, Jackson, Isaac, and Evie—who continue to teach me what it means to follow Jesus in the ordinary rhythms of daily life.

And most of all, to my wife, Emma—your steady love, wisdom, and belief in me have been a constant source of strength and inspiration. I dedicate this book to you.

INTRODUCTION

BEYOND BELIEF—PRACTICING THE WAY OF JESUS

"Are you saved?"

That was the main question in my conversation with an organ salesman.

While shopping in the mall, I heard a familiar tune: "Nothing but the Blood of Jesus." The music was coming from an organ in a nearby store. I walked in, approached the man playing, and said, "I grew up in church singing that song. Thanks for bringing back some good memories."

He smiled and asked, "Are you saved?"

I smiled back and said, "Yes. I'm actually a United Methodist pastor."

Without blinking, he repeated, "But are you saved?"

I chuckled as I walked away because while his comments felt pushy, they were not unfamiliar.

Growing up in a church where believing the right things was the measure of true faith, I had heard that kind of language many times before.

In that tradition, being "saved" carried a specific meaning. It all started with preaching "the truth" of the Bible, understood as the correct (literal) interpretation that proved a particular set of beliefs. The goal was for everyone to hear this truth, believe it in their hearts, and then respond by accepting Jesus as their personal Savior. Yet in my experience, accepting Jesus was less about being deeply transformed in love and more about submitting to the church's teaching authority and agreeing with a list of right beliefs. Of course, not everyone in that tradition lived this way. Many were sincere, faithful people. But I began to notice a troubling pattern: Right beliefs did not always lead to Christlike lives.

As I grew older, I was surprised to see that people who believed nothing like me often looked more like Jesus in their everyday lives than the exemplars in my church. Even more surprising was how some who proudly claimed all the right beliefs could still be just as judgmental, bigoted, angry, or greedy as unbelievers. This left me wrestling with a hard question: How could people hold all the right beliefs yet look so unlike Jesus in the way they lived? It wasn't just theological inconsistency I noticed; sometimes real pain hid behind Sunday smiles.

I had a friend growing up whose father was a leader in the church. He was a tough kid who often got into fistfights, and I assumed that was why he sometimes had bruises on his face or body. But one day I visited his house and saw his father shove him against a wall in anger. My friend looked terrified, and at that moment I realized where he was getting all those bruises. I went home that day realizing that you can be a "Bible-believing Christian" and embrace a pattern of life that looks nothing like Jesus.

As I got older, wrestled with God, and discovered a faith of my own, I became convinced that Christianity is much more than believing the right things. It is a way of life, rooted in love, that has the power to change us from the inside out. In Scripture, faith is trust, loyalty, and obedience. Abraham is called the father of faith—not because he had the right ideas about God, but because he trusted God enough to pack up and move to a land he had never even seen. The author of James reminds us that even demons "believe," but belief without action has no power to save (James 2:19).

The Gift and Danger of Belief

It's not that belief is bad or unimportant. In fact, we all begin with beliefs that are passed on to us from our families, our communities, our culture, and sometimes our churches. These beliefs are good in the way they help us make sense of life. They orient us in the world, help us find meaning in our experiences, and give us direction so we can take risks and move forward.

But here's the problem: When beliefs are never tested through practice, they either lose their power to shape our lives or harden into rigid ideologies that become harmful and even idolatrous.

The real power comes when we combine belief with practice and reflection. When we act on our faith within a diverse community of Christians and reflect together on what we're learning, the Holy Spirit works to question, stretch, correct, and deepen our beliefs so they more closely reflect the life and teachings of Jesus. This is an ongoing, dynamic process that leads to real transformation, not only in how we hold our beliefs but also in the way we see the world and live our everyday lives. But the process only works if both belief and action keep moving together.

I've learned this the hard way when it comes to forgiveness. For a long time, I believed forgiveness was simply a choice to let go and move on. That worked fine in theory, but when I tried it with people who had really hurt me, it fell apart. The anger didn't go away; it grew into deep resentments.

That failure forced me back to God. I prayed more. I studied Scripture. I talked with pastors, counselors, and trusted Christian friends. And slowly, something shifted. I still believed in forgiveness, but the way I believed began to change. I realized forgiveness isn't a one-time decision; it's a process. It means naming the wrong for what it is, setting new boundaries, and surrendering the anger day by day until judgment gives way to compassion. And along the way I discovered that forgiveness is not only something I choose to do; it's also a miracle God works inside of me.

Practicing forgiveness didn't make me give up my belief; it transformed it. My belief became deeper, more real, more faithful to Jesus. And as my belief changed, so did I.

But when we separate belief from practice, discipleship grinds to a halt. Knowing about Jesus is mistaken for following him. We can quote Scripture, say eloquent prayers, and give arguments for what we believe, while never forgiving an enemy, serving the poor, or defending the powerless. An obsession with information drains away the power of transformation.

The danger doesn't stop with individuals. An overemphasis on belief also weakens the church. When "being right" matters more than showing love, theological disputes divide rather than unite. Belief becomes a litmus test of who is "in" and who is "out." Instead of creating a community of love, churches risk becoming gatekeepers of correctness. Families are divided, friendships strained, congregations split—all in the name of holding the "right" beliefs. Yet the apostle Paul insists, "The only thing that counts is faith working through love" (Galatians 5:6 NRSVue).

When love is displaced by doctrinal scorekeeping, the result is anything but good news.

At its most dangerous, hollow belief creates a vacuum that invites distortion. When Christianity is reduced to religious teaching instead of a way of life, it loses sight of the God who humbled himself to share our humanity. The focus shifts from God's self-giving love to human power and position. We see this most clearly in the rise of Christian nationalism, where faith is hijacked by politics and used for status and control. Instead of shaping us to look more like Jesus, faith is recruited to bless the values of Caesar. The good news of grace and reconciliation is replaced by an ideology of exclusion and power. The result is people who claim the name Christian but look nothing like Christ.

The Power of Practice

But what if we focused on something deeper than belief, breaking free from the false gods it can create? If belief by itself can be twisted or misused, then practices, (what we can *do* with our faith) give us another path—a path that roots faith in action and opens us to God's transforming love.

When we focus on practices, faith stops being something to argue about and starts being something we live. Shared habits unite us across differences. Doing things like praying for our enemies, forgiving someone who wronged us, or serving a neighbor in need have a way of reshaping what we love. They don't just express faith; they form it as they form us.

The Christian tradition has long taught that what we do shapes what we love, and what we love shapes the way we live our lives. Furthermore, the practices that shape us (for good or bad) are never just private. We learn them and repeat them together. That's why the practices of the church matter so much. The church offers a different kind of community, one that forms us not by the habits of consumerism or nationalism but by shaping us into the likeness of Christ.

John Wesley would have agreed. For him, salvation was not a one-time event that secures a place in heaven, but a lifelong journey of becoming more like Jesus. Practices like prayer, meditating on Scripture, Holy Communion, and works of mercy were not extra credit for the ultrareligious. They were God's appointed instruments through which the Holy Spirit reshapes our loves and our lives. Wesley also taught that these practices are not merely individual but deeply communal. Christians grow in holiness together through shared accountability, encouragement, and service. Practiced in faith, the means of grace become the ordinary channels by which God's Spirit transforms believers into the likeness of Christ.

Scripture affirms the importance of practice too. Jesus does not only say "Believe my words" but "Follow me" (Matthew 4:19), and Christians were known as people of "the Way." The apostle Paul calls us to present our bodies as living sacrifices

(Romans 12:1), because our habits with the body shape the soul. Indeed, from Sabbath-keeping to prayer to forgiving enemies to caring for widows, orphans, and immigrants, the Bible is full of practices designed not merely to inform us but to transform us into the people of God. These are not secondary to faith but central to it.

God Transforms Us Through Practices

At the heart of Christian faith lies the conviction that we cannot transform ourselves. As Paul says, "God is the one who enables you both to want and to actually live out his good purposes" (Philippians 2:13). Human effort alone cannot conquer sin or reshape our hearts. Transformation is a work of divine grace.

Even though God is the only one who can transform us, God gives us practices that open our hearts to the work of the Holy Spirit. God's presence and power move through them to change us from the inside out.

John Wesley called these practices *means of grace*: visible signs, spoken words, or actions God has chosen to be ordinary channels of his transforming love. They are not magic, nor do they work automatically. They require faith, understood as a living commitment. When engaged with openness as an act of surrender, the Spirit works through them to awaken us to grace, to heal our disordered loves, and to re-form us into the likeness of Jesus.

Without such practices being rooted in a group of Christian friends, we fall back on self-effort or the influence of culture and other people to save us. As history and human experience make clear, this never works. But Christian practices slowly teach us to love as God loves.

In a world where Christianity is too often known for what it argues about or what it believes, one goal of this book is to think carefully about what Christians should do. In this way, I hope to reclaim the formative power of Christian practices through which God makes us more like Jesus.

Many books have been written on the classic spiritual disciplines: prayer, Bible study, fasting, worship. Those are important. But this book aims to widen the lens. It will help us see how everyday actions—some familiar, some surprising—can shape our hearts, reorder our desires, and lead to transformation.

Why I Wrote This Book

We live in a time when the church's witness is often compromised. Surveys show that many young adults associate Christianity more with judgment than with grace, more with division than with unity. Headlines too often portray Christians as people of anger and exclusion rather than love and mercy. Meanwhile, others quietly settle into a shallow, polite faith that avoids controversy but lacks the power to transform lives. Both distortions keep us from the abundant life God intends.

What the world longs for—what we long for—is a faith that makes a real difference, a faith that transforms us into people of courage, compassion, humility, and hope. That kind of faith doesn't come by accident. It comes by practice.

This conviction is what led me to author this book. In seminary and graduate school, I devoted myself to studying the core teachings of the Christian faith—work that has deeply shaped my life and identity. But in the church, I found myself sitting with grieving families, counseling couples in crisis, and walking alongside friends torn apart by politics. In those moments, what mattered most was not what I knew (or thought I knew) but what I did.

Pastoral ministry has shown me that while belief matters, it is not enough. In fact, the church's frequent focus on belief alone has sometimes produced serious distortions. Only intentional practices, rooted in a faithful reading of Scripture, can shape our hearts and make us more like Jesus. Without them, we are likely to remake Christ in our own image and slide more quickly into idolatry.

This conviction has only deepened as I've served diverse congregations that include both conservative and progressive Christians, and as I've watched my own denomination, The United Methodist Church, walk through a painful season of disaffiliation that has cost us about one-fourth of our congregations in the United States. These experiences have convinced me more than ever that what matters most is not arguing about beliefs but learning to live like Jesus even as disagreements remain. It is our practices—our habits of justice, mercy, grace, faith, and wrestling—that will hold us together, transform us, and bear witness to a watching world.

The book began as a summer sermon series and grew into something more—a vision of how new practices can lead to a transformed life in Christ. I hope you will use this book for personal spiritual growth or read it with others in a small group or Bible study. Pastors may also find it useful in shaping their own sermon series. However you use this resource, my hope is the same: that it helps you see the power of spiritual practices and invites you into a deeper journey of becoming more like Christ.

The Journey Ahead

This book unfolds as a series of practices—each grounded in Scripture and designed to form us more deeply into the image of Christ. The chapters follow a natural progression: beginning with our inner commitment, and then moving outward into the ways we live, love, and serve in the world.

In chapter 1, "Christians Practice Surrender," Jesus calls us beyond a shallow faith that costs little and changes nothing. Drawing from Luke 14, we see why discipleship demands wholehearted commitment and how this leads to the transforming practice of daily surrender.

Chapter 2, "Christians Practice Forgiveness," explores what it truly means to forgive an enemy and shows how forgiveness becomes one of the Spirit's most powerful tools for reshaping our lives into the likeness of Jesus.

From there, chapter 3, "Christians Practice Empathy," reveals that faith must move beyond belief into the way we treat people. Through the parables of the good Samaritan and the Pharisee and the tax collector, we see how pride and apathy close our hearts, while empathy and grace open us to action. Practicing empathy lays the foundation for the most visible expressions of Christ's love.

In chapter 4, "Christians Practice Mercy and Justice," we turn to Matthew 25:31-46 and discover that serving the vulnerable is not mere charity but an encounter with Christ himself. With grace-awakened eyes, God moves us outward in acts of mercy and justice that bring healing to a broken world.

Chapter 5, "Christians Wrestle with God," reflects on Jacob's long night of struggle in Genesis 32. Here we're reminded that faith is not about certainty but about holding on to God through doubt, pain, and unanswered questions. Wrestling with God is not a failure of faith but a vital part of discipleship—one that forms resilient, mature Christians who can bless the world even when they don't have all the answers.

Finally, chapter 6, "Christians Share Faith," turns to 2 Timothy 1:1-14 to explore how we pass faith from one generation to the next. Parents, grandparents, and the wider church family share responsibility for nurturing children and youth in the love of Christ, practicing faith in the everyday rhythms of family life. Unlike approaches that equate faithfulness with isolating children through rigid indoctrination, this vision invites us to cultivate authentic Christlike faith in our closest relationships.

Taken together, these chapters trace a path of Christian formation. The journey begins with deep commitment, moves into the home, and extends outward through empathy, forgiveness, mercy, justice, and honest wrestling with God. Along the way, we discover that discipleship is not simply what we believe but how we live lives shaped by the love, mercy, and grace of Jesus Christ.

Because this journey is about formation, not obligation, I want to be clear: This book is not about piling on more religious duties. It's about discovering how God's grace works through everyday practices to reshape our hearts. My prayer is that as you read, you won't just learn something new, you'll *do* something new. And in the doing, you'll find God forming you into the likeness of Jesus.

So I invite you to join me on this journey. Think of it as stepping onto a well-worn path where countless Christians before us have walked. Along the way, we will discover practices that open us to grace and shape us in love. My hope is that together we will move beyond abstract ideas into the grit and beauty of real life, learning not only what Christians believe but what Christians do.

CHAPTER 1

CHRISTIANS PRACTICE SURRENDER

Many years ago, I went through a difficult season of ministry. I was trying to lead through conflict, and it was tearing me apart. The strain was also spilling over into my family. At times it all felt overwhelming, and I found myself wondering if I had chosen the wrong vocation. Even as I tried to hold everything together, I kept busy with preaching, teaching, and counseling—but I wasn't tending to my own soul. I taught the Bible to others, but I wasn't spending much time letting it speak to me. I led worship, but I rarely experienced Sabbath rest. I encouraged people to seek Christian friends and accountability, but I didn't have those kinds of relationships in my own life. Eventually I hit a breaking point, drained and depressed, when I finally had to face the truth: My faith had become shallow.

At the urging of a friend, I went on retreat to the Monastery of the Holy Spirit in Conyers, Georgia. One evening, sitting alone in my room and practicing contemplative prayer, I was overwhelmed by a love unlike anything I had ever felt before. It's one thing to say "I believe God loves me." It is quite another to feel God holding you together when life seems to be coming apart. That moment reminded me of what faith was all about and renewed my calling. It gave me the strength to return to my congregation and keep loving them faithfully.

More important, it taught me that faith cannot survive without daily surrender—without opening myself to God's love and relying on that love to reshape me into the image of Christ. Everything else flows from this practice. Without that realization, and the changes it brought to my life, I probably would not be a pastor today.

My experience at the monastery opened my eyes to the truth that shallow faith cannot sustain us. And I discovered I'm not alone in this struggle. Even Jesus's own disciples wrestled with what it means to take faith seriously.

When Faith Is Shallow

One day, when Jesus told his disciples that he must suffer and die, Peter pulled him aside and protested: "God forbid, Lord! This won't happen to you" (Matthew 16:22). Jesus's response was stunning: "Get behind me, Satan" (v. 23). Then he turned to the others and said:

> *All who want to come after me must say no to themselves, take up their cross, and follow me. All who want to save their lives will lose them. But all who lose their lives because of me will find them. Why would people gain the whole world but lose their lives? What will people give in exchange for their lives?*
>
> *(vv. 24-26)*

This is the heart of the gospel: If you cling to your life—trying to secure safety and happiness by putting yourself first—you will lose it. But if you are willing to lose your life for Jesus, surrendering fully to him and walking in obedience to his way, you will discover a life rich with meaning, purpose, and joy.

This surrender is not a one-time decision of the mind. It is a daily practice. Every day, we choose again to put God first in how we speak, how we spend, and how we love. This first act of surrender is the foundation for everything else we will explore in this book. Without it, nothing else can take root, because discipleship begins with giving Jesus all of who we are. With each step, our surrender grows deeper and our transformation more complete. But without this kind of commitment, faith becomes fragile, unable to sustain all the other practices that shape us into the likeness of Christ.

So what does it really mean to take faith seriously? It can't just be about believing the right things or showing up at church once a week. Jesus is inviting us to something deeper: to put him first and to actually live out his way of life. When we practice what he teaches, our faith grows strong. But if we don't, it stays shallow and easily gets twisted into something it was never meant to be.

And that's where the danger comes in. In my years as a pastor, I've seen two distortions of faith. One is quiet: people who believe in God but admit their faith makes little difference in daily life. The other is loud: people whose faith has turned angry and combative, convinced they're defending God when they're really defending their own ideology.

On the surface, these two distortions seem as far apart as a whisper and a war cry. But in reality, the first often fuels the second. Shallow faith leaves a vacuum, and something will always rush in to fill it. In our day, that "something" is often nationalism—but beneath it all is the deeper problem of a hollowed-out faith.

The Danger of Shallow Faith

By hollowed-out faith, I mean a faith with no real commitment, especially when life gets hard. It might change a Sunday schedule, but not a life. It asks little, costs nothing, and leaves churches looking more like social clubs than places where enemies are forgiven, neighbors are fed, and outcasts are welcomed as family.

Shallow faith can be hard to see because it hides behind respectable habits. It's the person who comes to church every Sunday but does not open a Bible the rest of the week. The entrepreneur who brands his business as Christian yet cuts corners when it benefits the bottom line. It's the couple who prays before dinner but never seeks God's direction in the kind of decisions that matter most.

It's important to remember that this critique is not about perfection but direction. Real faith shapes how we speak when we are angry, what we do with unexpected money, how we treat the people who frustrate us most. It shows up when we bite our tongue instead of firing back in traffic or when we pause to pray before deciding how to use our tax refund. It's the patience we choose with a child who pushes our buttons or the generosity we extend when we'd rather play it safe. Real faith takes shape in these ordinary moments—small choices that reveal what really matters. And while living this way is not easy, the truth is clear: A faith that costs nothing will change nothing.

Jesus himself warns against shallow discipleship. In the parable of the sower (Mark 4), he describes seeds that fall on rocky ground. They spring up quickly but wither just as fast when trouble comes. This kind of faith is enthusiastic in the moment, but rootless when life gets hard.

He makes a similar point at the end of the Sermon on the Mount. After laying out his teaching on a range of things from anger and lust to forgiveness and generosity, he says, "Everybody who hears these words of mine and puts them into practice is like a wise builder who built a house on bedrock. . . . But everybody who hears these words of mine and doesn't put them into practice will be like a fool who built a house on sand" (Matthew 7:24-26).

The difference Jesus highlights between the builders is not between hearing and not hearing but between hearing and doing. Shallow Christianity listens to the words of Jesus yet fails to put them into practice. And when the storms of life come, that kind of faith cannot stand; the house collapses.

John Wesley, the founder of Methodism, warned about this kind of shallow faith too. In his sermon "The Almost Christian,"[1] he described people who lived moral, respectable lives and even spoke sincerely about God, yet had never been fully transformed by grace. His point was that it's possible to be religious and well meaning and still miss the fullness of life Jesus came to bring.

Dietrich Bonhoeffer, a German pastor and theologian during the rise of Nazi Germany, sounded a similar warning in the twentieth century. He is best known for resisting Hitler's regime, which eventually cost him his life. Bonhoeffer spoke about what he called "cheap grace"—forgiveness without repentance, Christianity without discipleship, grace without the cross.[2] He saw how this kind of shallow, comfortable faith left the church powerless in the face of evil. In Germany, this created a vacuum that was quickly filled by Nazi ideology; complacency opened the door for nationalism. In contrast to cheap grace, Bonhoeffer explains that following Jesus is more than going to church and believing the right things. It demands something real and sacrificial.

When we apply these lessons today, we are reminded that our faith requires real commitment because its goal is a radical transformation that impacts every area of life. It aims to change how we spend money, how we do our work, how we treat our families, and how we respond to those in need. It reshapes our values, our character, our ethics. Real faith does not simply tweak our behavior. It makes us a new creation (2 Corinthians 5:17).

Given the kind of commitment required for this transformation, Jesus tells us to count the cost before rushing into a decision to follow him.

Counting the Cost of Following Jesus

In Luke 14, we find Jesus traveling toward Jerusalem, attracting large crowds who were eager to see his miracles and hear his teachings. The energy is high, and expectations are building. And then he says something that stops everyone in their tracks:

> *"Whoever comes to me and doesn't hate father and mother, spouse and children, and brothers and sisters—yes, even one's own life—cannot be my disciple. Whoever doesn't carry their own cross and follow me cannot be my disciple."*
>
> *(Luke 14:26-27)*

Taken at face value, this sounds extreme and even offensive. But Jesus is not speaking literally. He isn't calling us to despise our loved ones. Rather, he is using hyperbole, an ancient teaching method used by rabbis to grab our attention and emphasize the seriousness of a point. And the point is this: If you want to follow Jesus, he must come first. Above your family. Above your money. Above yourself. Why? Because if God is not first in your life, then something else is—and that is what the Bible calls idolatry.

Since Jesus is asking so much of us, he tells us to count the cost before deciding to follow him, and to illustrate this point, he gives a short parable:

> *"If one of you wanted to build a tower, wouldn't you first sit down and calculate the cost, to determine whether you have enough money to complete it? Otherwise, when you have laid the foundation but couldn't finish the tower, all who see it will begin to belittle you. They will say, 'Here's the person who began construction and couldn't complete it!'"*
>
> *(Luke 14:28-30)*

The danger Jesus is highlighting is lack of commitment and follow-through—something we see in many areas of life. Marriages entered into too quickly, businesses launched without planning, career changes made on impulse. In the moment, it feels right. But when the cost sets in and the passion fades, people realize they acted without a solid foundation.

Faith works the same way. Becoming like Christ is not a quick fix but a lifelong renovation that requires steady habits of trust, surrender, obedience, and sacrificial love—habits that slowly reshape us into the image of Christ. Such a transformation demands solid commitment from the start, because only deep resolve will sustain us when life gets hard or when the demands of discipleship feel inconvenient. Without that commitment, it's easy to let go of the very rhythms that make us more like Jesus.

That's why Jesus urges us to begin with our eyes wide open by counting the cost. He isn't trying to discourage discipleship; he's trying to prevent us from beginning with a superficial commitment. Pointing to the image of an unfinished tower, he says: Don't do this with your soul. Don't start following me unless you have really thought it through. Discipleship is not easy, and it is not about good intentions. It is about a lifelong, all-in commitment to a particular way of life. And the only way it works is if you count the cost at the front end.

While counting the cost may feel daunting, it is not only about what we give up but also about the blessings we gain. Sometimes it helps to see what this looks like in real life. In my own congregation, I think of a couple who embodies this truth. After a trip to Nicaragua, they felt God calling them to serve the poor—not just on short-term mission trips but as a way of life. They chose early retirement from successful careers, traded the comfort of home in the United States for long seasons abroad, and one of them even trained as an EMT to serve as part of their community's only ambulance service.

By most standards, they made significant sacrifices. But when you talk with them, they light up as they tell stories of the people they serve, the lives they've seen change, the community that has embraced them. In giving up so much, they discovered more than they ever imagined—joy, purpose, and a deeper love for God and people.

This example shows that counting the cost of discipleship is really about going all in with Jesus. In the end, Jesus isn't after your money, volunteer hours, or votes; he is after your heart. He wants all of you. He wants you to love him above everything else, just as he loves you, and to make sharing that love with others the driving purpose of your life. That is the pathway to true joy.

Deep down, we all long for this kind of love. Every human heart yearns for a love that is total, committed, and sacrificial. That longing was placed in us by God, who uses it to awaken and draw us into his own love—so we can be transformed by it, love him back with our whole heart, and share it with others. God loves us all the way, and he wants us to love him all the way too.

This is the love I experienced at the monastery, which helped me go back and love a congregation divided by conflict. It is the love that my friends in Nicaragua experienced in the faces of the poor, which empowered them to continue sharing God's love in hard places. And it's the love that Jesus invites all of us to receive and extend to others. Not a partial, when-it's-convenient kind of love, but a wholehearted, all-in kind of love. And when we've been loved in such a way, how can we offer anything less in return?

This is why the practice of daily surrender matters so deeply. When we open our lives to God, he fills us with his love. In that love, the Holy Spirit supplies the strength we need to stay committed and to keep doing the things that make us more like Jesus. We cannot do this on our own. Surrender is the channel through which God's power flows to make it possible.

The Practice of Daily Surrender

At some point, we are all faced with a question: Have I truly counted the cost of following Jesus? Am I willing to go all in? Jesus makes it clear that anything less than full surrender will not bring the transformation that makes life truly good. But if we are willing to go all in, everything changes. We discover a love that heals, transforms, inspires, and fills life with joy.

If you have heard the call of Jesus to go all in, don't ignore it. Pay attention to what God may be saying to you and let it deepen your faith. This is not a call to add a bunch of extra religious obligations to your life, but an invitation to enter a life-changing relationship with God.

If you don't know where to start, consider a daily practice of surrender.

Surrender is not about passivity. It's not about resignation or abandoning responsibility. It's the acknowledgment that God is already present—offering grace, power, love, and guidance for today. We don't do things to make God show up; God is already here. Our task is to learn how to get out of the way.

Surrender means making space to reconnect with God's presence. It involves becoming receptive and opening our hearts so that God's life can flow into us and change us. It's about setting aside our ego so that Christ can live more fully through us: "I have been crucified with Christ and I no longer live, but Christ lives in me" (Galatians 2:20).

Surrender helps us keep our priorities straight by releasing control and putting God first. In practice, it's a way of resisting internal voices—our wandering thoughts, selfish desires, anxieties, and distractions—that pull us away from God and lead us into a self-focused life. It's also a way to push back against external voices that constantly demand our attention: news cycles, social media, cultural expectations, ambitions, and fears. Without this kind of resistance, all those voices become louder and drown out the quiet, small voice of God.

Surrender is how we create space for God. It is a quiet, deliberate effort to listen for God's voice so the Spirit can flow into us—giving us a broader and deeper perspective, reminding us of who we are and whose we are, and providing clear direction for the day ahead.

With so many pressures and distractions pulling our attention away from God, surrender isn't something we do once and forget; it's something we return to daily, sometimes even multiple times a day.

Different practices can help us live this out, but two have been especially vital in my own spiritual life: prayer and connection.

First, I try to start each morning with the full Serenity Prayer, letting each line shape my posture for the day:

God, grant me the serenity
to accept the things I cannot change;
courage to change the things I can;
and wisdom to know the difference.

Living one day at a time;
enjoying one moment at a time;
accepting hardships as a pathway to peace;
taking, as Jesus did, this sinful world
as it is, not as I would have it;

trusting that You will make all things right
if I surrender to Your will;
so that I may be reasonably happy in this life
and supremely happy with You forever in the next.
Amen.

Then I prayerfully meditate on Scripture using the practice of *lectio divina* (sacred reading). This is something I learned from the monks at the Monastery of the Holy Spirit.

Lectio divina starts with a slow, prayerful reading of Scripture. I choose a book of the Bible—such as the Psalms, a Gospel, or an Epistle—and read it very slowly, listening with expectation for God to speak to me through the text. When a word, image, or verse touches my heart or catches my attention, I stop and sit with it, sometimes repeating it slowly to let it sink in.

Then I prayerfully consider why this particular word or verse speaks to me and reflect on it in concrete, personal ways. This often reveals where I need encouragement, insight, correction, or growth. Journaling can be helpful here.

Next, I respond to God through honest, conversational prayer, openly sharing my feelings. I end this prayer by choosing how I will live differently in response.

Finally, I sit in silence for five or ten minutes, letting go of words, thoughts, and agendas, gently releasing distractions as they arise. The goal isn't productivity but presence, trusting that God delights in spending unhurried time with me. I find it helpful to gently focus on my breathing. As I inhale and exhale, I remember that the Hebrew word for Spirit is *ruach*, which also means "breath" or "wind." From the very beginning of Scripture, God breathes the breath of life into humanity. That image isn't just about creation long ago; it's a reminder that every breath we take is upheld by God's ongoing gift of life.

In a world filled with noise, silence can feel unnatural—even uncomfortable—yet it's in that quiet space that my fears, anxieties, and compulsions surface, and I can offer them to God. Over time, as I rest in God's presence, my motives become clearer, my hurts are healed, and my desires are gradually reshaped in the image of Christ.

This way of praying through Scripture is a powerful act of surrender.

Finally, as I move through my routines and responsibilities, I return to the short version of the Serenity Prayer—the first four lines—or a simple one-sentence prayer of surrender whenever I feel myself grasping for control or slipping back into old patterns. Each repetition becomes a quiet reminder to let go and surrender again.

In addition to prayer, I surrender daily by staying connected to Christian friends. Sometimes that means meeting in person to surf or grab lunch, but most often it's a phone call. My goal is to make at least one call each day to share honestly about how I'm doing, seek new perspective, get support, and ask for accountability.

Time and again, these conversations have helped me stay committed to Jesus, simply because a friend reminded me who I am in Christ and encouraged me to act as my true self. Along the way, I've gained wise counsel, felt deeply loved, and received the kind of accountability that keeps me on track. (Commitment is hard to maintain without encouragement and accountability.)

These daily connections are simple, but they have become one of the most powerful ways I practice surrender to God.

I've also discovered that the loving power released through daily surrender has a shelf life of about twenty-four hours, much like manna—the mysterious, sweet-tasting food that kept the Israelites alive in the wilderness. In Exodus 16, after God delivered Israel from slavery in Egypt, he provided manna each morning and quail in the evening. The people were told to gather only enough for that day, with the exception of the day before the Sabbath when they could collect twice as much. This wasn't simply about food storage; it was a lesson in trust. God was teaching them to resist the impulse to hoard and instead rely on his promise day by day: Each morning, fresh manna will be there.

That same practice mirrors what it means for us to take faith seriously. We don't receive a lifetime supply of spiritual strength all at once. God calls us to daily surrender—opening our hearts to him again and again so he can give us exactly what we need just for today.

For me, this has become a lifeline. Every day I neglect to practice surrender, my awareness of God begins to fade. I gradually get lost in my own thoughts and routines. I become increasingly preoccupied with my concerns. I become more self-focused without realizing it. I drift away from God's presence and from my true center. I lose sight of my purpose: to glorify God and to become more like Jesus. And I lose the power to do what God is calling me to do. That is why surrender must be daily.

While prayer and connection are what work for me, something different may work for you—and that's okay. What matters is developing a daily practice of surrender that keeps you rooted in God and connected to Christian friends.

This simple rhythm opens the door to real transformation. It's the foundation for everything else. And remember: God never asks us to go all in without first going all in for us. His love is total, committed, and sacrificial—and that love is what makes our surrender possible.

CHAPTER 2

CHRISTIANS PRACTICE FORGIVENESS

Forgiveness is one of the most powerful ideas in the Christian faith, but it's also one of the hardest to practice. I think of a friend whose story shows just how difficult and healing true forgiveness can be.

Emmett grew up feeling abandoned by his father. His parents met when they were seniors in college and married when his mom became pregnant, but the marriage did not last. Not long after Emmett was born, they divorced.

His mother made some significant changes, worked hard, and gave her son as much stability and love as she could. A close bond grew between them. His father kept living as if nothing had changed, drifting in and out and spending little time with his son. He wasn't completely absent, but he was unreliable—there for some birthdays and milestones but missing many others. Promises often went unkept, leaving Emmett unsure whether he could trust his dad. Over time, sadness hardened into anger, and anger into resentment.

Years later, after Emmett married and had children, his father wanted to be part of his grandchildren's lives. That would only be possible if Emmett forgave him. His Christian faith kept pressing him in that direction. He knew God had forgiven him and called him to forgive others, yet forgiving his father felt almost impossible. Over time, though, two things began to soften his heart.

The first was his own children. His father's failures were not their fault, and he didn't want to repeat the cycle by denying them a relationship with their grandfather. To his surprise, even though his dad had not been there for him as a child, he became a reliable and loving presence for his grandchildren.

Second was his father's willingness to admit past failures and apologize. As Emmett considered his own shortcomings as a parent, he began to see his father with more grace and less judgment. He wasn't perfect either, and one day he would need forgiveness from his children. That humility opened his heart to the possibility that his father's apology was sincere and that reconciliation could begin.

Forgiveness did not erase the pain, but it allowed compassion to take root. And as compassion grew, so did forgiveness. Grace opened a future that anger could never create.

Emmett's story reminds us how deeply we all long for forgiveness, and how hard it can be for us to extend it. His story is not unique. We all wrestle with forgiveness in one way or another. But over the years, I've learned that forgiveness is essential to any enduring relationship. People will hurt us, and we will hurt them. Without forgiveness, our marriages collapse, our families fracture, our friendships end, and even our churches split. Without forgiveness, nations unravel in cycles of violence and revenge. Without forgiveness, our own souls become prisons, locked in bitterness, shame, and regret.

So where do we find forgiveness deep enough, strong enough, and lasting enough to change us? The Christian faith insists that forgiveness begins with God in Jesus Christ. But it does not stop there. The forgiveness we receive becomes the forgiveness we extend, and as we practice it, it reshapes us—little by little—into the image of Christ.

Jesus Forgives and Calls Us to Forgive

Forgiveness is a core practice of Jesus in the New Testament. He reveals how God forgives us and then calls us to forgive others.

When it comes to understanding the nature of God's forgiveness, few stories are as powerful as the parable of the prodigal son. Many have heard this story before, but there's value in slowing down and letting it speak to us again.

Jesus tells the story of a man with two sons. One day, the younger son makes a shocking request: "Father, give me my share of the inheritance" (Luke 15:12). In first-century Palestine, the family normally distributed the inheritance after the father's death. To demand it early was deeply dishonorable, effectively saying, "I wish you were dead—now give me what's mine." Shocking as it is, the father grants the request.

The younger son takes the money, leaves home, and squanders everything in extravagant living. He spends until nothing is left, and when a famine strikes, he finds himself destitute. Hungry, humiliated, and reduced to feeding pigs, he realizes just how far he has fallen. In desperation, he begins to rehearse a speech:

"Father, I have sinned against heaven and against you. I no longer deserve to be called your son. Take me on as one of your hired hands" (vv. 18-19). With this plan in mind, he begins the long walk home.

Much to his surprise, while the son is still far off, his father sees him, is filled with compassion, and runs to meet him. In the ancient world, dignified men did not run, but this father throws aside all convention, races to his son, and embraces him. Before the young man can even finish his carefully rehearsed confession, the father interrupts, calling for the best robe, a ring, and sandals—symbols of full restoration to family status. He orders a feast to celebrate, "because this son of mine was dead and has come back to life! He was lost and is found!" (v. 24).

What matters most in the story is not the son's attempt to earn his way back but the father's gracious embrace. With this focus, Jesus paints a vivid picture of what God is like: not a distant judge waiting to condemn but a loving parent longing to welcome his children home. Forgiveness is not a grudging cancellation of debt but a joyful welcome.

This is Jesus's portrait of God: a parent whose mercy is not measured by the depth of the offense but by the depth of love. Forgiveness, in this vision, is not merely a moral obligation but an act of love that brings the dead to life and creates the conditions for restored relationships. The father's joy reveals the heart of God, and Jesus invites us to see in this story a God whose forgiveness overflows with abundance. This is where forgiveness begins: in the lavish grace of God. And the more we receive it, the more it reshapes us into people who can extend the same grace to others.

Jesus not only reveals the heart of God's forgiveness; he calls his followers to share it. This comes into sharp focus in Matthew 18 when Peter asks Jesus a very practical question: "Lord, how many times should I forgive my brother or sister who sins against me? Should I forgive as many as seven times?" (v. 21).

We can all relate to Peter's question. Surely there must be a limit to how many times we forgive someone who keeps hurting us. But Jesus gives a shocking reply: "Not seven times, but, I tell you, seventy-seven times" (v. 22 NRSVue). He isn't telling us to keep an exact record of wrongdoing so that on the 491st offense we can finally take our revenge. No, he is telling us to forgive without keeping score. And as he so often does, he drives the point home by telling a parable.

The story begins with a master who wants to settle accounts with his servants. He calls for a servant who owes him an impossible sum: ten thousand talents. To grasp the scale, one talent was about twenty years of wages for a laborer. Ten thousand talents would be billions of dollars in today's terms, more than any ordinary person could repay in multiple lifetimes. When the servant cannot pay, the master orders that he, his family, and his possessions be sold. The man falls on his knees and begs for mercy: "Please, be patient with me, and I'll pay you back" (v. 26). Of course, the promise is absurd; no amount of time could make repayment possible. Yet, in a shocking act of mercy, the master cancels the debt entirely and sets him free.

The story should end there, with a man overwhelmed by grace. But Jesus continues. The same servant, freshly released from an unpayable debt, goes out and finds a fellow servant who owes him a hundred denarii, about three months' wages. Pocket change compared to what he had just been forgiven. Yet he seizes him by the throat and demands repayment. His fellow servant falls down and pleads for patience, using almost the same words he himself had spoken. But the forgiven servant refuses and throws the man into prison until the debt is paid.

Other servants, outraged by the injustice, report the matter to the master. The master summons the first servant and says: "You wicked servant! I forgave you all that debt because you appealed to me. Shouldn't you also have mercy on your fellow servant, just as I had mercy on you?" (vv. 32-33). In anger, the master hands him over to be punished until the debt is repaid. Jesus ends the parable with this sober warning: "My heavenly Father will also do the same to you if you don't forgive your brother or sister from your heart" (v. 35).

The lesson is clear: Those who have received mercy must extend mercy. We cannot expect God to forgive us if we refuse to forgive others. God's forgiveness is undeserved and unlimited, and Jesus expects his followers to mirror that same forgiveness in their own relationships.

Whereas the parable of the prodigal son shows us the heart of God's forgiveness, the parable of the unforgiving servant reveals the expectation that disciples live out that forgiveness with others. Forgiveness is not simply a gift to receive; it is a way of life that flows from God's mercy into human relationships. The more we practice this way of life, the more it forms us in the image of Jesus, who embodies God's forgiving love.

Jesus Practices and Embodies Forgiveness

It is one thing to talk about forgiveness and another to live it. Jesus sets an example for us by doing both. In addition to teaching about forgiveness, he shows it in concrete encounters, embodying God's mercy in his words and actions. In doing so, he makes it clear that forgiveness is not just an abstract idea but a way of life.

Early in his ministry, Jesus heals a paralyzed man brought to him by friends (Matthew 9:1-8). But before he heals his body, Jesus speaks to a deeper need: "Be encouraged, my child, your sins are forgiven" (v. 2). The religious leaders are scandalized and accuse him of blasphemy. Who can forgive sins but God alone? To prove his authority, Jesus heals the man physically, showing that the forgiveness of sins and the restoration of health belong together. Jesus embodies forgiveness as God's power to make people whole.

Jesus does something similar at a dinner hosted by a Pharisee. A woman with a sinful reputation enters uninvited. Overcome with emotion in the presence of Jesus, she began to weep, and her tears fell on his feet. In an act of humility and devotion, she wiped them with her hair, kissed them, and anointed them with expensive perfume (Luke 7:36-50). The Pharisee is appalled, but Jesus receives her act of devotion and declares, "Your sins are forgiven" (v. 48), teaching us that the act of being forgiven restores our dignity and expands our capacity to love.

When a woman is caught in adultery, religious leaders drag her out into the public square before Jesus, demanding that she be stoned to death according to the law (John 8:1-11). Instead, Jesus turns the tables and says, "Whoever hasn't sinned should throw the first stone" (v. 7). One by one, the accusers leave until only the woman remains, terrified and humiliated. Then Jesus extends grace by saying, "Neither do I condemn you. Go, and from now on, don't sin anymore" (v. 11). In that moment, he shows that love triumphs over the strict demands of justice and that forgiveness makes possible a new future—not defined by failure, but by the hope of a second chance.

Hanging in agony on the cross, Jesus continued to live what he preached by praying for his executioners: "Father, forgive them, for they don't know what they're doing" (Luke 23:34). In the very moment of unspeakable injustice, he offered grace. If ever there was a time for vengeance, it was here—but instead of striking back, Jesus absorbed the violence and broke the cycle of retaliation.

Finally, after his crucifixion and resurrection, Jesus forgave Peter, one of his closest disciples, for denying him. A few days earlier, Peter had openly declared that he would never stop following Jesus, even if it meant death (Mark 14:29; John 13:37). Yet on the night of Jesus's arrest, when the pressure mounted, Peter crumbled. As Jesus was taken into the courtyard of the high priest for questioning, Peter waited outside by the fire. Three separate times, people recognized him and asked, "Aren't you one of his disciples?" Each time Peter denied it, insisting he did not even know Jesus. Immediately after the third denial, a rooster crowed, and at that moment, Jesus turned and looked straight at Peter. Overcome with shame, Peter exploded in tears and ran away (Luke 22:54-62).

Yet the story does not end in despair. After the Resurrection, Jesus encounters Peter on the shores of Galilee and asks him three times, "Do you love me?" (John 21:15-17)—mirroring the three denials. Each time Peter says yes, and each time Jesus responds with some variant of "Feed my sheep." As we might expect by now, Jesus forgives Peter and restores their relationship. But even more surprising, Jesus recommissions him as a leader in the church. Instead of casting Peter aside, he entrusts him with the care of the Christian community, showing that forgiveness not only heals what is broken but can also reshape our life's mission.

In all these examples, Jesus does not just preach forgiveness; he practices it. He enacts what he proclaims, thereby rooting the church's practice of forgiveness in his own example. To truly forgive, then, is to forgive like Jesus. And since Jesus reveals what God's forgiveness looks like, to forgive others is to extend the kind of forgiveness we have received from God.

It's important to remember that forgiveness always begins with God. We cannot generate it on our own; we can only pass on what we have first received. As Paul writes in Ephesians 4:32: "Be kind, compassionate, and forgiving to each other, in the same way God forgave you in Christ." Forgiveness always starts with the grace of God in Jesus. When we receive that gift, it transforms us. And when we practice forgiveness with others, we not only extend grace, but we are also reshaped into the image of Jesus himself. In this way, forgiveness is both gift and formation, mercy received and mercy shared.

In all of this, we see that forgiveness is not optional for Christians; it is the very heart of our imitation of Christ. Jesus reveals God's mercy, calls his followers to forgive without limit, and embodies forgiveness in his own life, death, and resurrection. To follow him is to live in the rhythm of receiving this gift and extending it to others. To forgive as Jesus forgives is not merely a choice but the defining mark of Christian life.

What Forgiveness Is Not

But what does forgiveness look like in everyday life? This is an important question because forgiveness is one of the most misunderstood words in the Christian vocabulary. Many of us feel overwhelmed by the command to forgive because we don't truly grasp what it means. If we are to forgive as God forgives, we must first clear away the confusion.

Forgiveness is not shrugging off or excusing wrongdoing. Sometimes it's fine to overlook small offenses. If someone bumps into you in a crowded theater, the best response is usually to keep walking. But serious wrongdoing cannot be ignored or dismissed with phrases like "It wasn't a big deal" or "I know you didn't mean it." Sin is real, and forgiveness requires naming it truthfully rather than pretending it doesn't matter.

Forgiveness is not denying or suppressing our true feelings. Too often we think that to forgive means we must bury our anger or pretend the hurt doesn't sting. But real forgiveness requires honesty. Just as we must name the offense truthfully, we must also acknowledge the emotions that come with it. Anger, grief, sadness, even rage—these are real, and they have to be brought into the light. Only when we process our feelings in healthy ways, through prayer, trusted conversation, or counseling, can our hearts be prepared to truly forgive. Skipping this step only drives the pain underground, where it festers and makes forgiveness harder.

Forgiveness does not enable abuse. It doesn't mean staying in harmful situations, pretending everything is fine, or giving people permission to keep hurting us. Enabling harm under the pressure to "stick together" is not forgiveness; it is self-destruction.

Forgiveness does not erase all consequences. A thief may still serve time. A spouse may still face divorce. A child may still need correction. Major violations of trust often change the nature of a relationship. Forgiveness releases a person from guilt, but it does not cancel responsibility or remove the need for new boundaries.

Forgiveness is not revenge. Jesus rejected the old logic of "an eye for an eye" (Matthew 5:38) not because justice no longer matters but because retaliation multiplies harm. Forgiveness refuses the cycle of payback and opens the door to healing and reconciliation.[1]

Forgiveness in the Christian Tradition

At its heart, forgiveness means telling the truth about what happened, condemning the wrong, and then releasing the person from the debt their actions created. It is saying, *Yes, you hurt me. Yes, it was wrong. But I will not carry the weight of resentment forever or insist that you suffer in return.* We do this whether the other person asks for forgiveness or not.

This does not mean pretending there was no wrongdoing or simply going back to business as usual. Forgiveness does not erase the offense. But instead of demanding payback, it lays down our right to balance the scales. More than figuring out what the relationship will look like afterward, forgiveness is about a change of heart. It has the power to free both the offender and the offended from being chained forever to that one act, the victim to resentment and the victimizer with guilt.

Forgiveness is costly because it absorbs pain instead of striking back. When someone wrongs us, the instinct is to retaliate, to make them hurt the way they hurt us. But forgiveness interrupts that cycle. It chooses grace instead of revenge.

We know forgiveness is taking root when something shifts inside us. Where there was only judgment, we begin to feel compassion. Where there was bitterness, we sense the stirrings of mercy. Forgiveness doesn't erase memories, but it changes how we carry them.

In the Christian story, forgiveness begins with God. In Jesus, God names the truth about human sin, bears the cost of that sin on the cross, and releases us from its crushing debt. And just as God forgives us, God calls us to forgive others. Practicing forgiveness does not come easily. It takes honesty, courage, and time. But when we walk this path, God reshapes us from the inside out. We become people who reflect the mercy we have received, people who look a little more like Jesus.

Why Forgiveness Is So Hard

All of this sounds good in theory, but what happens when the offense causes serious harm? What about betrayal, abuse, or cruelty? How can we forgive when our hearts are shattered?

I think of a woman who grew up in a home marked by alcoholism and domestic violence. Her father would spend the family's grocery money on booze then come home and beat her mother. Once, he punched her in the face so hard that she was knocked unconscious, and the children feared she might be dead. Her father also ruthlessly beat her brothers. Sometimes her mother would also drink and whip the kids with a heavy leather strap used to polish and sharpen a straight razor. The combination of poverty and abuse left deep wounds that scarred all the children for life. In situations like this, forgiveness might be impossible in this life.

Still, forgiveness is an ideal we can strive for; it is a key aspect of Jesus's teachings as well as a path that most often leads toward healing for both the people doing the forgiving and those being forgiven. But even for offenses that don't have truly life-altering consequences, forgiveness can be extraordinarily difficult.

The first reason for this is our deep sense of justice. From childhood we are hardwired for fairness. When our kids were young, my wife would buy the other sibling a small gift for the birthday party, so no one felt left out. I often questioned this, but she reminded me how sensitive kids are to perceived injustice. And this is not something we outgrow. A basic sense of fairness is part of what it means to be human.

This means that when we perceive an injustice, our natural response is to balance the scales. When someone hurts us, that desire to restore justice can sound like "He's got to pay for this!" or "She needs to feel what I felt!" We may not call it revenge, but our hunger for fairness can quickly turn into anger because forgiveness can feel like a guilty person is getting off scot-free.

But the gospel insists that forgiveness is not opposed to justice. Rather, it is rooted in God's justice. On the cross, God did not dismiss sin. God judged it fully and then bore the judgment

Godself. Forgiveness is not saying justice does not matter. Again, it involves naming and condemning the wrongdoing, accepting the natural consequences, and rethinking the boundaries in the relationship. But it also involves trusting that God's ultimate justice has been accomplished in the cross of Christ, and just as God has freely forgiven me, I can now forgive you. Ultimately, love always rises above justice in an economy of grace.

The second reason forgiveness can be so difficult is the depth of the pain we carry. Abuse and trauma leave lasting marks on our bodies, minds, and souls. When the pain is raw, the command to forgive can even sound cruel.

This is why forgiveness cannot be reduced to sheer willpower. We cannot simply grit our teeth and say "I forgive you" and expect it to carry real meaning. Forgiveness is always a miracle of grace. Only God can truly forgive sins, and in a mysterious way, when we forgive others, it is God who is doing the forgiving through us. Paul expressed this truth when he said, "I have been crucified with Christ and I no longer live, but Christ lives in me" (Galatians 2:20). To forgive is to let Christ live through us—to allow his Spirit to do in us what we cannot do by ourselves. Some wounds are so deep that no human being can forgive on their own. But what is impossible for us is possible with God, who works forgiveness in us as a miracle of grace over time.

Forgiving is also hard because it is a process. Earlier we saw how Jesus tells us to forgive without limitation—seventy times seven. Reflecting on my own experience, I think Jesus said this because forgiveness is rarely a one-time act. We must keep choosing it and practicing it over and over again.

Like many of you, I carry wounds from someone in my family who has hurt me deeply, not just once but many times. I have spent decades in counseling working through the ongoing pain of that relationship. Each time I find the strength to forgive, another wound reopens, and I must forgive again. Over the years, this cycle forced me to set stronger boundaries. Eventually, after a heartbreaking argument, I made the difficult decision to have no contact with this person until he took responsibility and made amends. That final act of letting go carried significant consequences for my family relationships, but it gave me the space I needed to truly forgive him *one more time.*

Still, forgiveness did not end there. Painful memories and waves of anger resurface, and when they do, I must forgive again—not seven times, but seventy times seven. Only by returning to that process do I find healing, freedom, and the slow reshaping of my heart into the image of Christ. Forgiveness is never quick or easy. It is a lifelong journey of refusing to let bitterness have the last word and allowing grace to transform us into a different kind of person.

In cases like this, God calls us to surrender our anger in prayer. We ask God to heal our wounds, soften our hearts, and even give us the desire to forgive. Sometimes this work takes years. Sometimes it requires therapy, counseling, or spiritual direction. Forgiveness rarely comes quickly, but God is patient. God does not rush us; God walks beside us until our hearts are ready. And as we keep surrendering and opening ourselves to God's transforming love, God works forgiveness within us. Through the Holy Spirit, God makes possible what we cannot do on our own, leading us into freedom and joy.

This helps us make sense of Jesus's command to love our enemies. It is one thing to forgive a friend who lets us down, a spouse who disappoints us, or a child who disobeys. But Jesus goes further: "You have heard that it was said, *You must love your neighbor and hate your enemy.* But I say to you, love your enemies and pray for those who harass you" (Matthew 5:43-44).

How is this even possible? It's not by pretending our enemies are our best friends. Not by continuing to subject ourselves to mistreatment or abuse. We love our enemies by forgiving them, which means naming and condemning the wrong, reconfiguring the relationship in response to the offense, and setting new boundaries that make it possible to rebuild trust. If rebuilding trust is not possible or safe, then the only way to love them may be to release them from our desire to retaliate, walk away, and entrust them to God in prayer.

The command to love our enemies by forgiving them stirs up all kinds of resistance. It provokes fear: *What if they hurt me again?* It provokes anger: *They don't deserve mercy!* It awakens powerlessness: *If I let go of my resentment, I'll have no control.* And yet, this is central to the Christian life. When we set others free through forgiveness, we set ourselves free as well, free to live and to love like Jesus and enjoy the fruits of abundant life.

Wrong Reasons to Forgive

Since forgiveness can be so hard, it's easy to twist it into something it is not.

We do not forgive our enemies to irritate them. Oscar Wilde is credited with the quote, "Always forgive your enemies; nothing annoys them so much." That line may get a laugh, but forgiveness is not a passive-aggressive way to vent anger or balance the scales. It's not a weapon disguised as grace. Nor do we forgive to appear morally superior. Pride can twist forgiveness into a performance: *Look how virtuous I am compared to my enemy.* This only deepens division. And we don't forgive primarily to feel better, even though forgiveness often does bring freedom and healing.

The deeper motive is our longing to be like Jesus and to make the world more like God wants it to be. Christians forgive enemies because God forgave us when we were enemies of God (Romans 5:10). One reason why the gospel is good news is because God's forgiveness is not limited to a select few who are in some way worthy. Christ died for *all*—friends and enemies alike. If God withheld forgiveness until we deserved it, we would all be lost. But God forgave us while we were still sinners (Romans 5:8), thereby empowering us to forgive others, even the unrepentant.

The Goal of Forgiveness

While it is true that repentance is not a condition for extending forgiveness, it is a condition for reconciliation, which is the ultimate goal. Forgiveness aims to restore a broken relationship, and it is often the act of forgiveness itself that opens the door to this possibility. Forgiveness can tear down walls of hostility so that friendship might be restored. It can also create space for people to confess what they would otherwise hide. If I know that admitting my sin will not result in condemnation but in grace, I am more likely to tell the truth. This is what God's forgiveness did for us in Jesus, moving us from enemies to friends.

But sometimes reconciliation is not possible in this world. Sometimes the best we can do is forgive from a distance and entrust the offender to God. But even then, forgiveness bears witness to the truth of the gospel: that God's grace is greater than sin, that love is stronger than hate, and that the cross has broken the cycle of vengeance.

Forgiveness as Transformation

So far, we have said a great deal about how forgiveness affects the offender. But as a core practice in Christianity, it also transforms the one who forgives.

When we forgive, we release others from guilt and debt. But in doing so, we also release ourselves. Bitterness is like drinking poison and expecting the other person to die. Resentment corrodes our souls. When we cling to anger, we chain ourselves to the past. But forgiveness sets us free. It does not erase the memory of what happened, but it loosens the grip that memory has on us. It allows us to remember without being consumed.

This is why Jesus says in Matthew 6:14-15, "If you forgive others their sins, your heavenly Father will also forgive you. But if you don't forgive others, neither will your Father forgive your sins." These words are not meant as a threat of divine vengeance but as the description of a spiritual reality. Forgiveness is not a private possession we can hoard; it is a gift meant to flow. When we refuse to forgive, we block the very grace we ourselves depend on. Forgiveness is like a river—living water that comes from God, passes through us, and refreshes others. If we dam it up, it grows stagnant and loses its power to transform. But when we allow it to flow, it not only brings life to others but also cleanses and renews us.

Forgiveness also transforms us into the image of Christ. Each time we forgive, we reflect something of Jesus, and over time the practice of forgiveness reshapes our character. We become more merciful, more compassionate, more patient. We learn to see others not merely as offenders but as fellow sinners in need of grace.

I've seen this in my own life as a parent. Not long ago, I bought an expensive new TV for our family room. This was the only spot where my daughter could play virtual reality games, which required her to wear a headset that completely covered her eyes. Less than two months after setting it up, she accidentally hit the screen and broke it.

She came into my room in tears, terrified to tell me what had happened, expecting anger. In the past, she would have been right. But over the last several years, I've been working—with my wife's encouragement—to soften my reactions and practice grace with my kids. Sometimes I've succeeded, and sometimes I've failed.

That day, by God's grace, I was able to pause, take a deep breath, and say, "Evie, it's okay. I know it was an accident. We all make mistakes, and it's going to be all right." She couldn't believe my response and even offered to give all the money in her piggy bank, $17.23, to help pay for it. I smiled and said, "Why don't we just adjust the VR settings so it doesn't happen again?"

I won't pretend it was easy. A part of me still felt angry hours later, and I was tempted to fall back into my old pattern of lecturing. But I didn't. Practicing small acts of forgiveness over the years had changed my heart. When this bigger test came, I was able to respond with grace. Looking back, I'm far prouder of that choice than I ever would have been of scolding her. Because in that moment, I caught a glimpse of Jesus reshaping me.

A Community of Forgiveness

As with all the practices we are considering in this book, forgiveness is not only personal but also communal. The church is meant to be a community where we practice forgiveness regularly. In baptism, we are washed in the forgiving love of God, dying to sin and rising to new life in Christ. In Holy Communion, we remember that Christ's blood was poured out for the forgiveness of sins, and we come to the table reconciled to God and to one another. In our basic pattern of worship, we regularly practice forgiveness through prayers of confession and repentance. In these ways and more, forgiveness is not an abstract idea but becomes embodied in the life of the community. And in daily life, God calls us to bear with one another, forgive grievances, and work toward reconciliation. A church that does not practice forgiveness is not a true church, because forgiveness is at the core of the gospel.

When forgiveness becomes the norm in a Christian community, it forms us into people who embody grace in the world. We become a living testimony that reconciliation is possible, that enmity does not have to be the last word, that Christ is risen and sin is defeated.

Forgiveness as the Way of Christ

Forgiveness is hard. Sometimes it feels impossible. And yet it's at the heart of what Christians do. We forgive because God forgave us. We forgive because forgiveness is the only way we can heal broken relationships. We forgive because bitterness destroys us, but grace sets us free. We forgive so God can reshape us into the image of Christ.

Some of you reading this may carry deep wounds. Maybe you were betrayed by someone you trusted. Maybe you suffered abuse. Maybe the one you need to forgive has never admitted their wrongdoing. Forgiveness does not mean excusing sin or removing natural consequences. Nor does it mean reconciliation is always possible. But forgiveness does mean refusing to let the offense define you and the other person forever.

You may also struggle to forgive yourself, living under the crushing weight of regret. We are often our own worst critics, punishing ourselves for mistakes that we cannot undo. Hear the good news: God has *already* forgiven you in Christ and empowers you by the Holy Spirit to receive that gift for your own transformation.

And remember, we don't forgive ourselves or others by mustering up enough willpower. It is something God does in us and through us. Our task is to stay close to Jesus, to surrender our pain and anger to him, and to allow the Spirit to flow through us so that we might be healed and set free.

At the end of the day, forgiveness is not about forgetting the past. It's about allowing God to open us to a new future.

Forgiveness is not something we practice alone; it's something we walk out together as followers of Jesus. It's not about weakness but the power of God's grace. It is not about excusing wrong but declaring that our mistakes will not have the last word. When Christians forgive, we bear witness to the God who forgives. And in forgiving, we live into the central truth of the gospel: Forgiveness begins with God's grace in Jesus, and as we practice it, God reshapes us into his likeness.

May you find the courage to release what chains you, the grace to forgive what wounds you, and the freedom of Christ reshaping your heart in love. Pray for the desire to forgive. Pray for the strength to forgive. Pray for the miracle of forgiveness to flow through you. And as you do, remember this: Forgiveness is not only a gift you give to others; it is also the way God sets you free, gives you abundant life, and makes you more like Jesus.

CHAPTER 3

CHRISTIANS PRACTICE EMPATHY

It's More Than a Feeling

When the phone rang, I could hear the concern in Judy's voice. "Pastor Mark, Jimmy and I would like to come and see you in the office." She didn't offer details, only that it needed to be soon. When they sat across from me the next day, I learned why. Jimmy had just received an unexpected cancer diagnosis, and they were waiting for more tests to determine the stage and what treatment might look like.

I was deeply concerned for Jimmy, but I had walked with many parishioners through cancer before, and most of those journeys ended with the hopeful news of remission. So I prayed with Jimmy and Judy, asked them to keep me updated, and assured them of my ongoing support.

Within a few weeks, Judy asked me to make a home visit. When I walked in and saw Jimmy in his recliner, I almost didn't recognize him. His condition had declined so quickly that he could barely speak. They were still trying to process news no one is ever prepared to hear: "There's nothing more we can do."

Hospice had been called, home health workers scheduled, but the goal was simply to keep Jimmy comfortable. Both of them knew the end was near, and they wanted their pastor to help them draw strength from their faith.

While I do my best to care for each person in my congregation, pastors inevitably grow closer to some more than others. Jimmy and Judy were among those for me. As longtime members of the church, they worked in our memorial garden every week, the same place where they laid their daughter to rest years earlier, after a deadly asthma attack. Their sweet spirits, servant hearts, and constant encouragement endeared them to me. So when I saw Jimmy fighting to stay awake in his chair and the pain in Judy's eyes, it broke my heart.

Though I struggled to find the right words, I held a safe space where they could express their pain without fear of judgment. I opened my heart and gave them my full attention. By listening with compassion and asking gentle, open-ended questions, I invited them to share even more deeply. Before I left, I placed my hand on Jimmy's shoulder and prayed for them both. I told him I loved him, and then walked outside with Judy. She shared a little more of her fear, and after reassuring her of my love, I gave her a hug and told her she could call me anytime.

Just a few weeks later, Jimmy passed away.

Looking back, what was most healing during those visits was not anything I said but rather the gift of empathy—not as a passing wave of emotion, but as a steady practice of attention and presence. It was the deliberate choice to be vulnerable by listening to their pain without making myself the center of attention, holding a safe space for honest reflection, sitting with them in the struggle, and connecting with their pain without trying to offer easy solutions. Empathy understood in this way is more than a feeling; it's a spiritual practice that trains our hearts in love and shapes our lives to look more like Jesus's.

What Empathy Is—and Isn't

Empathy is a word we hear often, yet it easily gets reduced to sentimentality or emotion. To recover its depth as a Christian practice, we need to define it carefully, and a good starting point is to distinguish it from similar concepts like sympathy and compassion.

Sympathy is when we *feel for* someone. We may genuinely care about what happens to them, but we stay at a distance from their pain. A friend loses a loved one, and we send a quick sympathy card between appointments. An acquaintance posts online about losing a job, and we comment, "You're in my thoughts and prayers." These gestures are thoughtful, but they can still leave the other person feeling unseen or alone.

Empathy goes deeper; it's when we *feel with* someone. The word comes from the Greek root *em* ("in") and *pathos* ("feeling" or "suffering"), meaning "in suffering with." It's not just noticing hurt from a distance but choosing to deeply connect with another's perspective and pain. Practicing empathy means creating safe space for honest expression, listening with genuine attention, and imaginatively stepping into another's experience so that their suffering touches our heart. It's to stay present in another's struggle rather than retreating to the safety of our own comfort.

Compassion grows out of empathy. As we connect with another's perspective and pain, we often experience a desire to help in some way. We see this repeatedly in the life of Jesus. Whenever he is described as feeling compassion, it always leads to concrete action: He heals the sick, feeds the hungry, or teaches the lost. Compassion is not merely a feeling; it's love that rolls up its sleeves.

All three—sympathy, empathy, and compassion—are important, but empathy is the crucial bridge between distant pity and active love. Without empathy, sympathy stays at a safe distance, and compassion never finds its legs. Empathy is what allows us to put ourselves in another person's shoes so that we can be present in their suffering. It is the practice of opening our hearts, holding safe space for their struggle, refusing to look away, and letting their pain matter enough to change how we see them and respond.

With these important distinctions, we can clear away some common misunderstandings. Empathy is not mere sentimental indulgence, like rushing in to say things like "Everything happens for a reason" or "God won't give you more than you can handle." Such words may ease our own discomfort but do little to help a person who is hurting. Nor is empathy emotional fusion without boundaries, where we absorb another's pain so completely that we lose ourselves or our ability to be of real help. And empathy is not uncritical moral approval, as if standing with someone in their suffering means we must endorse everything they say or do.

True empathy is a disciplined, discerning, and Christlike practice. It requires wisdom and healthy limits, along with the courage to remain present amid suffering without collapsing into it or turning away.

Empathy in the Life and Teachings of Jesus

Understanding empathy in this way can be helpful, but seeing it embodied brings it to life. In Jesus, we find empathy not as theory but as practice—love that listens, feels, and acts for the sake of others. Nowhere is this more clearly seen than in his interactions with people throughout the Gospels. And when we pay close attention to these encounters, we discover something striking: Jesus never condemns anyone for being too compassionate, too merciful, or too loving. His harshest critiques were always directed at religious leaders who placed rigid interpretations of holy texts, strict purity codes, moralistic rules, and exclusionary boundaries above the needs of hurting people—something that can happen in any religion. Again and again, Jesus confronts the ways belief without empathy distorts the human heart.

We see this clearly in a sharp critique of some Jewish religious leaders in Matthew 23: "How terrible it will be for you legal experts and Pharisees! Hypocrites! You give to God a tenth of mint, dill, and cumin, but you forget about the more important matters of the Law: justice, mercy, and faith" (v. 23). These men tried to follow the religious rules down to the last detail but missed the heart of God's commands: love. Without empathy, their religion became a stumbling block to true faithfulness.

In contrast, Jesus teaches that true faithfulness involves practicing empathy as a concrete expression of love. One of the clearest examples of this is the parable of the good Samaritan

(Luke 10:25-37). It begins with a religious expert testing Jesus by asking, "What must I do to inherit eternal life?" (v. 25 NRSVue). When Jesus pointed him back to the law, loving God with your whole being, and loving your neighbor as yourself, the man pressed further: "And who is my neighbor?" (v. 29). He wanted to know who counted and who didn't, who deserved his compassion and who could be excluded.

Jesus responded with a story of a man beaten, stripped, and left for dead on the road. Two religious leaders passed by without stopping, unwilling to risk impurity, interrupt their duties, or complicate their plans. Then came a Samaritan.

In Jesus's day, Samaritans were despised by Jews and treated as outsiders, even enemies. Yet this Samaritan, the last person anyone expected to stop, saw the wounded man's suffering and allowed it to touch his heart. He didn't settle for pity at a safe distance. He crossed the barrier of prejudice, moved toward the man's pain, and allowed himself to be stirred by mercy for someone he might otherwise have avoided. That is empathy—the courage to see another's suffering and step into their reality. And from that empathy grew compassion, which moved him to act: He bandaged the man's wounds, lifted him onto his own animal, brought him to an inn, and paid for his care.

This story shows that empathy is not just feeling sorry for someone. It is the bridge between noticing suffering and responding with love. Without empathy, the Samaritan might have simply walked by like the others. Instead, he entered into the wounded man's struggle and, moved by compassion, helped in specific ways that cost him time, energy, and resources.

When Jesus finished the story, he asked, "Which one of these three was a neighbor to the man who encountered thieves?" (Luke 10:36). The answer was obvious: "The one who showed mercy." Jesus then said, "Go and do likewise" (v. 37). In other words, if you want to live out the greatest commandment—if you want to love God with your whole being and to love your neighbor as yourself—then you must practice empathy. And not only with friends or people like you, but with anyone you encounter who is in need, regardless of race, religion, or relationship.

Jesus understood that apathy (emotional indifference and disengagement) hardens the heart. It trains us to look away, to feel less, to pull back—not just once, but again and again—until avoidance becomes a habit. Over time, compassion narrows. We start to reserve our care only for those closest to us, those we think are "deserving," those who will not cost us too much. Our love becomes smaller, more conditional, and less like the love of Jesus.

In contrast, practicing empathy expands our love and helps us to obey the Greatest Commandment. The priest and the Levite may have thought they were being faithful, and no doubt they valued love in theory. But their apathy revealed how religion without compassion is little more than performance. The Samaritan, on the other hand, showed that true faithfulness is not found in rigid rule-keeping but in the practice of empathy, which moves us to help.

In addition to teaching about empathy, Jesus practiced it throughout his ministry. Take, for example, his encounter with a man who had a withered hand (Mark 3:1-6). On the Sabbath,

Jesus entered the synagogue and noticed the man's suffering. The religious leaders were watching closely because they wanted to see if Jesus would heal him. In their eyes, healing counted as work, and working on the Sabbath was a violation of their rules. Jesus called the man forward and asked, "Is it legal on the Sabbath to do good or to do evil, to save life or to kill?" (v. 4).

When the onlookers refused to answer, Jesus stepped into the man's suffering with empathy and, stirred by compassion, healed him. But the leaders? Jesus looked at them with both sadness and anger because their rules had become more important than love. Their rigid interpretation of Scripture had blinded them to the suffering of the person right in front of them.

We see something similar in Jesus's encounter with a woman caught in adultery (John 8:3-11). Once discovered, the religious leaders drag her out in public and quote Scripture as a justification to execute her. Jesus responded to their inhumanity and judgmental attitude by saying: "Whoever hasn't sinned should throw the first stone" (v. 7). One by one they walked away. In the end, Jesus looked at the woman not with condemnation but with compassion: "Neither do I condemn you. Go, and from now on, don't sin anymore" (v. 11). Jesus condemns the religious leaders for using Scripture as a weapon to shame and destroy, while showing the true way of love—empathy that listens and feels and compassion that restores.

Again and again, Jesus's empathy opened the door to compassion. His willingness to enter people's suffering moved him to act with mercy and power. This was not an occasional response but the consistent pattern of his life and ministry. Even more, as we will see in the following discussion, Jesus's practice of empathy revealed and embodied the very heart of God.

Incarnation as Divine Empathy

The most powerful expression of empathy in the Christian faith is found in the mystery of the Incarnation. This central event reveals that God is not distant or detached from the human story but draws near to us in Jesus, entering fully into the human condition. God does not watch from afar while we struggle with pain, sin, and death. Instead, God comes close, living among us, sharing our humanity, and taking our suffering into God's own life.

This is what makes the Incarnation so breathtaking: God does not only feel *for* us but also *with* us. As the embodiment of God the Son, Jesus knows hunger and fatigue. He weeps at the tomb of his friend. He experiences rejection, betrayal, and loneliness. On the cross, he even bears the full weight of human suffering and sin, an unimaginable act of divine empathy. God in Christ enters into the darkest places of human experience and refuses to abandon us there.

This means that we are saved by divine empathy, not as a fragile feeling but as an act of love strong enough to carry the full weight of human suffering and death. In the cross of Jesus, God takes our suffering and death into himself and overcomes it with love.

Consequently, we cannot follow Jesus while distancing ourselves from the suffering of others. To follow him means loving others indiscriminately by practicing empathy in our everyday lives—moving toward the pain of others, bearing it with them, and embodying God's presence in the middle of it. This is why the apostle Paul urges us to "carry each other's burdens" (Galatians 6:2), for in doing so we imitate Christ. And this is why empathy is not merely an impulse but a Christ-shaped discipline that teaches us to love in concrete, tangible ways.

Yet even with such a clear witness in Jesus, many still struggle to see empathy as something good and necessary in the life of faith. Throughout history, some have mistaken empathy for weakness or moral compromise. Naming these misunderstandings helps us recognize more clearly what genuine, Christlike empathy looks like.

Barriers to Empathy

In recent years, some voices in evangelical and fundamentalist circles have gone so far as to call empathy a sin. They warn that if we allow ourselves to feel the suffering of another person, it might cloud our judgment, weaken our moral resolve, or tempt us to compromise biblical truth.

But these critiques rest on a shallow definition. They portray empathy as nothing more than unstable emotion, prone to distortion and manipulation. Christian empathy, however, cannot be reduced to sentimentality. Rather, it's the deliberate practice of opening our hearts, listening with care, and holding space for another without losing ourselves. Far from weakening us, it strengthens us for love.

As we noted earlier, nowhere in Scripture does Jesus condemn having too much compassion or love. His rebukes always fall on those whose hearts had grown hard. To reject empathy is to align not with Christ but with the Pharisees, who elevated rules over people and lost sight of God's mercy.

Biblically and theologically, empathy lies at the very center of the way of Jesus. It reveals his humility, his courage, and his love. And for those who truly follow him, empathy becomes central for us as well. It's what enables us to see others through the eyes of Christ, to move toward people in their suffering, and to live out the greatest command to love God and our neighbors.

But even when we know empathy is central to the way of Jesus, we often resist it for more personal reasons.

Many of us know what it feels like to be overwhelmed when our efforts to help people fall short. Without realizing it, we begin to live by an unspoken motto: "If I can't fix it, I won't feel it." To shield ourselves, we instinctively choose not to enter into another's struggle, and this makes it easy to lose sight of their humanity. But Jesus never asked us to solve every problem or erase every ounce of pain. Rather, he calls us to be present in ways that make God's love real. While empathy doesn't fix everything, it tries to ensure that we don't have to suffer alone.

That's what I was trying to do when I sat with Jim and Judy in the final weeks of his life. I couldn't heal his body or take away the fear they both felt as the end drew near. But there was still tremendous value in simply sitting with them, listening, praying, and reminding them that they were not alone. That, too, is the work of Christ. Just as Jesus entered into our suffering and bore it with us, we can do the same for others.

This is the power of empathy. It works not by solving every problem but by opening a space where love can be felt, where isolation is broken, and where God's presence can be known in the midst of pain. This deep connection with others is also where we find the wisdom and motivation to act in ways that truly help.

Another way we avoid empathy is through blame. By saying "They made bad choices" or "It's their own fault," we reduce a person to a problem and give ourselves permission not to care. But Jesus never allowed blame to become a barrier to love. He consistently saw people not as problems to dismiss but as children of God worthy of dignity and love.

Both fixing and blaming are ways of protecting ourselves from discomfort, but they also shrink our capacity for love.

Empathy as a Spiritual Discipline

Although many people reduce empathy to emotion, in Christianity, it's a spiritual disciple like prayer or fasting. Through intentional practice and repetition, empathy becomes a habit of the heart that forms us in the image of Christ. Just as prayer tunes our hearts to God, empathy tunes our hearts to our neighbor. And just as fasting reshapes our desires, empathy reshapes our perspective, teaching us to see others not as problems to avoid but as people to love.

Empathy is a discipline of attention and presence, of choosing, again and again, to pause and notice, to listen without rushing to fix, to name another's pain without making it about us. It is learning to read Scripture from the perspective of the marginalized, so that we hear the voices of those who are often overlooked. It is practicing imaginative prayer, asking God to help us see the world through another's eyes. It is deliberately entering spaces of discomfort instead of shielding ourselves from it. And it is cultivating discernment and boundaries, so that our empathy is sustainable and life-giving rather than exhausting or consuming.

As we read the New Testament, three simple words seem to capture the way of Jesus: Notice. Stay. Love. This is the pattern of empathy as a spiritual discipline. We notice by letting ourselves see and feel the pain around us. We stay by refusing to run away when it becomes uncomfortable. We love by allowing our presence to become an expression of Christlike compassion.

When we approach empathy in this way, it shapes both the person who is hurting and the one who chooses to hold their pain. By training ourselves in empathy, we learn to love more like Jesus—steadily, attentively, and with a presence that reflects God's own presence with us.

Spiritual Transformation

When we practice empathy, it transforms us. It softens our hearts. Left unchecked, apathy hardens the heart and trains us to look away. But empathy breaks the grip of apathy and empowers us to enter another person's suffering. Our hearts become more tender, more open, more able to reflect the love of Jesus. Instead of avoiding pain, we learn to stay present with it. Rather than numbing ourselves or turning away, we begin to see that love is found in moving closer, not farther away.

Empathy also dismantles prejudice. It's easy to stereotype or dismiss someone from a distance, but when we sit with them in their struggle, the labels begin to dissolve. We no longer see an addict, an immigrant, or a stranger. We see a human being made in the image of God. Empathy retrains our vision so that we see people as God sees them.

As we've already seen, practicing empathy is one of the ways the Holy Spirit conforms us to the image of Christ, teaching us not only to love in word but also in presence. When we suffer with others, we are drawn into deeper communion with Christ, who suffers with the world. And something beautiful begins to happen—compassion grows, and humility deepens. This is the slow, steady work making us more like Jesus.

Empathy also lays the foundation for compassionate action. It is what gives us the right motivation for works of mercy and justice. Without empathy, our efforts to serve can become mechanical, self-serving, or driven by guilt. But when our actions flow out of empathy, they are rooted in love.

Empathy also creates the space where wisdom can emerge. When we listen and stay present with people, we begin to discern what kind of help is actually needed. It guards us from rushing in with quick fixes and trains us to act in ways that truly honor God and the person in front of us. Finally, empathy shapes the judgment we need for faithful engagement. It helps us know when to comfort, when to challenge, when to act, and when to simply be present.

Empathy opens our eyes, fuels our motivation, and grounds our discernment. In the next chapter, we will explore how this transformation leads us to serving the poor, the vulnerable, and the outcast through concrete acts of mercy and justice.

Walking the Way of Love

Empathy is a gift to embrace and a practice to cultivate. It is one of the central ways the Holy Spirit shapes us into the image of Christ and connects us with the life of God. It enlarges our hearts, deepens our faith, and draws us closer to the God who came near to us in Jesus.

I saw this truth in Jimmy and Judy's living room during his final weeks of life. I couldn't cure his cancer or take away their grief, but I could share their burden by sitting with them, listening, praying, and reminding them they were not alone. That is the work of empathy. It doesn't erase suffering, but it ensures people don't have to bear it alone. It takes some of the suffering out of the suffering. And in that space, God's presence becomes real and tangible.

This is the call of Christ: to open our hearts, refuse to look away, and step into another's story. It will not always be easy, and it will not solve every problem or remove every pain. But it will change us. And it will create space where love can be felt, where isolation is broken, and where Christ himself can be known.

While this may seem like a daunting task, as with the other practices in the book, we can begin small. Pay attention to the people right in front of you. Listen without rushing to fix. Hold space for someone's struggle without making it about yourself. Let yourself feel with them, even if all you can do is be present.

You don't have to solve the world's problems. You only have to do what Jesus did—notice, stay, love. And when you do, Jesus is already there, transforming both you and the one who suffers. And here is the good news: You never do it alone. Christ goes with you. The Spirit strengthens you. Even the smallest acts of presence make God's love known. So take courage, lean in, and love big!

CHAPTER 4

CHRISTIANS PRACTICE MERCY AND JUSTICE

Glimpsing Jesus

One Sunday after worship, I noticed a man sitting quietly in the back of the sanctuary. He waited until everyone left before approaching me. "My name is Jason," he said. "I was wondering if you could get me a tarp or a sleeping bag. A storm destroyed my tent, and I have nothing to keep me dry."

I had a few appointments that afternoon but told him I could meet around five o'clock. Later that day, I called his flip phone to let him know I was heading to Walmart. He had already walked to a nearby park and said he could meet me there.

I bought him a sleeping bag and met him in the parking lot. After handing him what would be his only protection against the elements, I offered a prayer and walked back to my car. As I was driving away, I caught a glimpse of him hobbling off, his face twisted in pain as blisters on his feet rubbed against his worn shoes.

I was overwhelmed with sadness because it was like watching Jesus himself disappear into the woods. In that moment, I felt God's presence wash over me.

Over the years, I've seen Jesus show up repeatedly in moments just like that one with Jason. Each encounter has been a window into grace. I saw Jesus in a disabled man demanding cab fare from emergency room staff after being discharged into a thunderstorm. I saw Jesus in the desperate eyes of a mother staying with her three children in our fellowship hall, clinging to the hope of finding a home. I saw Jesus in Alex, a homeless man living in the woods beside a busy Nashville highway, asking only for a new pair of boots so he could walk to the next town.

In each of these moments, grace didn't come from solving all the problems, but from showing up with empathy and care, recognizing that Christ was somehow present in the encounter.

Perhaps you've seen Jesus too—in the man at the intersection holding a cardboard sign or in the woman trudging off the beach at sunrise with all she owns in a plastic bag. In these moments, God isn't simply trying to stir our pity but reveal God's presence amid brokenness and despair. When we recognize Christ in the faces of the poor, the vulnerable, and the outcast, the Holy Spirit awakens us to God's love breaking into ordinary life through acts of mercy and justice.

The problem is that too often we miss it. Most of us aren't indifferent to the pain of others; it's just that life moves so quickly and the weight of responsibility leaves us exhausted. We hurry from one task to the next, falling behind and feeling guilty for not spending enough time with the people we love most. Emotionally fatigued, we start to shield ourselves from what we don't want to feel. But the gospel interrupts our hurry and worry. And when we slow down long enough to truly see another human being, we catch a glimpse of God.

Seeing Through the Eyes of Christ

In Matthew 25, Jesus tells the parable of the sheep and the goats. It's the last of three short stories that he shares to help us see what truly matters to God. He begins with a vivid scene: All the nations gathered before the Son of Man, a divine figure from ancient prophecy who represents Jesus reigning with God's authority as the world's true king and judge. Like a shepherd separating his flock, he places the sheep on one side and the goats on the other. The division isn't based on wealth, power, belief, or social standing, but on how each person responded to the needs of others.

To the sheep on his right, he says:

> *"I was hungry and you gave me food to eat. I was thirsty and you gave me a drink. I was a stranger and you welcomed me. I was naked and you gave me clothes to wear. I was sick and you took care of me. I was in prison and you visited me."*
>
> *(Matthew 25:35-36)*

To the goats on his left, he says the opposite:

> *"I was hungry and you didn't give me food to eat. I was thirsty and you didn't give me anything to drink. I was a stranger and you didn't welcome me. I was naked and you didn't give me clothes to wear. I was sick and in prison, and you didn't visit me."*
>
> *(vv. 42-43)*

Both groups are surprised because neither of them remembers ever seeing Jesus in these kinds of circumstances. "Lord," they ask, "when did we see you hungry and feed you, or thirsty and give you a drink?" (v. 37). He responds, "I assure you that when you have done it for one of the least of these brothers and sisters of mine, you have done it for me" (v. 40). With these words, Jesus so fully identifies with the poor, the vulnerable, and the outcast that how we treat them reflects how we treat him.

This story turns our normal religious assumptions upside down. It tells us that faith is not primarily about what we believe or the religious rituals we perform but about how we love. The ultimate test of faith, according to Jesus, is not found in words but in compassion lived out in real life, especially toward those who can give us nothing in return.

The goats in this parable are not condemned because they were especially cruel but because they did not see what truly matters to God: empathy and compassion. The real question posed by this story is not, What will happen after we die? but, How do we see the vulnerable among us?

Contrary to some evangelical teachings, this parable isn't meant to scare the hell out of us but to awaken us to God's value system. It's not about divine retribution; it's about divine revelation.

The story shows that those who live in love are already taking part in God's kingdom, while those who close their hearts align themselves with worldly kingdoms corrupted by sin, evil, and death. Jesus is teaching that we pledge our loyalty to one or the other by how we respond to the person right in front of us.

Spiritual Sight

This is what the parable is really about: seeing differently. According to Jesus, the difference between those who were called righteous and those who were not had nothing to do with holding the right beliefs but with how they saw the poor, the vulnerable, and the outcast. The distinction was not a matter of information but of spiritual sight awakened by grace.

That's why Jesus often used apocalyptic language to describe God's kingdom. Scholars remind us that when the Bible speaks of beasts, angels, final judgment, or the end times, it isn't offering a literal snapshot of the future. The word *apocalyptic* means "to uncover" or "to reveal." These passages were written to help people see differently—to lift the veil on ordinary life and show that God is still at work, even when that presence is hard to recognize. Rather than predicting what will happen someday, apocalyptic writing unveils what is happening right now: the hidden reality beneath all the noise of human power and ambition, and how God's love and justice remain the ultimate forces shaping history.

When Jesus speaks of the coming of the Son of Man and the judgment of the nations, he is peeling back the facade of worldly success and power to show what is real: the hidden presence of God among "the least of these." Through apocalyptic vision, we come to see that those whom the world overlooks—the hungry, the poor, the prisoner, the stranger—are precisely the people in whom we encounter God. In a real sense, to serve the poor is not only to bring Jesus *to* them but also to meet Jesus *in* them.

John Wesley described this grace-enabled way of seeing as *spiritual senses*. Just as we perceive the physical world through our natural senses, the Holy Spirit gives us new faculties for perceiving the divine presence in the world around us. These spiritual senses allow us to see Christ where others see only a problem, to hear the cry of the poor as the voice of God, and to feel the tug of compassion as a movement of the Holy Spirit. Without this spiritual vision, we can go through life numb to the suffering around us. With it, our hearts come alive, and the line between faith and action begins to disappear. Seeing as God sees draws us into loving as God loves. And that love, once awakened, manifests itself in action.

From Empathy to Action

In chapter 3, we explored empathy as a spiritual practice—a disciplined way of being present with another person in their suffering. More than emotion, it's the interior work of attention and presence that trains our hearts in love. Yet empathy is not an end in itself. Its true purpose is to move us toward compassion.

Rightly understood, compassion is love awakened by empathy and expressed through action. While empathy allows us to enter another's pain and perspective, compassion steps forward to serve with humility. In this way, empathy becomes the inner form of compassion; it shapes our hearts to act not out of guilt or pride but out of love strengthened by grace. The two are inseparable: Without empathy, compassion loses depth and becomes performance; without compassion, empathy stalls in sentiment and does not bear fruit. This is where the Christian life becomes visible, not in belief alone but in embodied love. The inward grace that attunes us to another's pain finds outward expression in self-sacrificial service.

When we practice empathy, God reshapes our hearts so we can see others through the eyes of Christ. When we act to help others, God aligns our daily living with the way of Jesus. Our hands and feet become instruments of his compassion in the world. Both belong together, because fully formed love moves in two directions: It attends faithfully to the suffering of others and acts courageously to bring healing and hope.

As we will see in the following discussion, compassionate action takes two forms. Acts of mercy respond to immediate needs, and acts of justice confront the systems that create those needs. Together they point us to the heart of our calling as followers of Jesus.

Mercy: The Heart of Love

Mercy is the spontaneous, Spirit-led movement of the heart to help someone in their moment of need. Jesus showed us what this looks like when he healed the sick, fed the hungry, and welcomed the outcast. In those moments, he didn't fix every system or solve every problem. He simply responded with presence, compassion, and love.

This is the way I helped Jason. I couldn't fix his homelessness or heal his wounds. But I could meet him in the parking lot, buy him a sleeping bag, offer a prayer, and remind him he wasn't alone.

Mercy doesn't always change someone's circumstances, but it changes the experience of suffering. And that change is not one-sided. Mercy transforms the one who gives as much as the one who receives. When we act mercifully, we resist the urge to see people as problems to be fixed and begin to see them as beloved children of God. In that moment of shared humanity, the Holy Spirit draws both the servant and the served a little closer to the heart of Christ.

Feeding the hungry, visiting the sick, and caring for the imprisoned are tangible ways we love our neighbors. And when we do these things in faith, they bear witness to God's love in the world and become more than gestures of human kindness. They become means of grace, channels through which God's transforming love flows both to others and back to us.

In these moments, we don't simply do a good deed; we take part in the self-giving love of God that sustains all creation—the same love revealed in Christ and poured out by the Holy Spirit. As we extend mercy, we are drawn more deeply into that divine life. The grace that moves through us also works within us, shaping our hearts to mirror the compassion of Jesus. In such acts, we are both agents and recipients of the love that sustains the universe and moves it toward the restoration of all things.

Yet mercy, as vital as it is, is only half the heartbeat of divine love. The other half is justice—acts that seek not only to relieve suffering but to right what is wrong.

Justice: The Public Face of Love

Acts of mercy are essential expressions of God's love, but disciples of Jesus are also called to confront the unjust systems that cause suffering. If we feed the hungry but never ask why people lack access to food, we risk reinforcing the very patterns that keep them hungry. If we offer temporary shelter but never ask why affordable housing is out of reach, we risk accepting policies that keep people trapped in homelessness.

This is where justice enters the picture. Justice asks not only how to relieve pain but also how to address its deeper causes. It aims to reorder society's structures so that all people can flourish.

Justice in the Prophets

The Old Testament prophets understood this well. They looked beyond the corruption and inequity of their day to envision a world renewed by God's justice and peace. Isaiah, for example, paints a beautiful picture of what life looks like when we live according to God's reign:

> *No more will babies live only a few days, or the old fail to live out their days. . . . They will build houses and live in them; they will plant vineyards and eat their fruit. . . . They won't labor in vain, nor bear children to a world of horrors, because they will be people blessed by the Lord.*
>
> *(Isaiah 65:20-23)*

In that vision, every part of life is made whole. Children grow up healthy and loved. Families have food, shelter, and meaningful work. People grow old with dignity and peace. This is not a utopian fantasy; it's a picture of God's will for all human beings.

The prophet Micah points to a similar vision when he says, "He has told you, human one, what is good and / what the Lord requires from you: / to do justice, embrace faithful love, and walk humbly with your God" (Micah 6:8). For him, we cannot separate truth faith from the pursuit of justice because God measures our devotion by how we treat the most vulnerable.

Amos proclaims that truth with even greater force, condemning religious rituals that ignore the suffering of the poor. Speaking on behalf of God, he says:

> *I hate, I reject your festivals;*
> *I don't enjoy your joyous assemblies. . . .*
> *But let justice roll down like waters,*
> *and righteousness like an ever-flowing stream.*
> *(Amos 5:21, 24)*

For these prophets, justice is not an abstract ideal or exercise in partisan politics; it's the public shape of love—the way mercy gives rise to social, cultural, and economic fairness. To love God, they insist, is to work for a world shaped by justice, peace, wholeness, and the flourishing of all creation.

Jesus and the Kingdom of God

Jesus stood squarely in this prophetic tradition. In his first sermon, he proclaimed:

> *The Spirit of the Lord is upon me,*
> *because the Lord has anointed me.*
> *He has sent me to preach good news to the poor,*
> *to proclaim release to the prisoners*
> *and recovery of sight to the blind,*
> *to liberate the oppressed,*
> *and to proclaim the year of the Lord's favor.*
> *(Luke 4:18-19)*

Jesus carried forward God's mission by casting anew the vision of the prophets. He proclaimed, embodied, and inaugurated the kingdom of God. When Jesus spoke of this Kingdom, he wasn't describing a distant heaven where people go after death but announcing God's reign breaking into the present world—a new order of love, justice, and peace that stands against every empire built on fear and greed.

In first-century Palestine, to speak of a "kingdom" was to use language with unmistakable political implications. The Roman Empire ruled by military power, extracting taxes from the poor and enforcing loyalty to Caesar, who was called "Lord and Savior." So when Jesus came preaching "the good news of the kingdom of God" (Luke 4:43 NRSVue), he was declaring that God—not Caesar—is the true King. The world already had plenty of rulers, but Jesus proclaimed a different kind of reign: not one established by violence or wealth but by justice, mercy, and truth. His message offered hope to the oppressed and posed a direct threat to the systems that profited from injustice.

In addition to preaching the kingdom of God, Jesus enacted it in his life and ministry. He cured the sick, healed people with disabilities, gave sight to the blind, and cast out enslaving spirits. His miracles were not simply displays of power; they were signs that God's justice was arriving in real time. He also confronted the more complex forces that kept people down—power structures that kept certain people on the margins, purity laws that divided communities, and economic systems that crushed the poor.

One of the clearest examples of this came toward the end of Jesus's life, when he entered Jerusalem for the last time. Pilgrims filled the city as they came to celebrate Passover, the great festival of Jewish liberation. When Jesus walked into the temple—the very heart of Israel's religious, economic, and political life—he saw the outer courts filled with merchants and money changers. Pilgrims had traveled long distances to worship, and the law required animal sacrifices. Because travelers couldn't easily bring livestock with them, merchants sold approved animals so people could take part in temple worship. In many ways, these services made obedience possible.

Yet something had gone wrong. What may have started as a practical accommodation seems to have created an opportunity for exploitation. Prices could be inflated. Access to worship could become expensive. The machinery of religion, even when based on legitimate needs, had begun to burden the very people it was meant to serve—especially the poor. In that crowded court, Jesus saw not just commerce, but a distortion of God's house and God's heart.

Seeing this, Jesus overturned their tables and drove them out, quoting the prophet Jeremiah: "My house will be called a house of prayer. But you've made it a hideout for crooks" (Matthew 21:13, quoting Isaiah 56:7 and Jeremiah 7:11).

This wasn't an emotional knee-jerk reaction, but a deliberate act of prophetic protest. Like Isaiah, Amos, and Jeremiah before him, Jesus confronted the corruption of both temple and empire, declaring that God's house must serve all people, not enrich the few. In that moment, he exposed the way religion and politics often join forces to protect power instead of advancing mercy and justice.

For the religious authorities, this was irreverent. For the Roman occupiers, it was dangerous. A man who claimed that

God—not Caesar—was king, who disrupted temple commerce during a national festival, and who drew crowds of poor and oppressed people was a political threat.

If we understand Jesus's temple disruption as a prophetic protest, then it was his passion for justice that got him killed. The Romans crucified him not because of his acts of mercy, but because he violated the Roman model of peace through force and stood against the false gods of power, privilege, and empire.

The kingdom of God that Jesus proclaimed was and is a direct threat to every system—religious, economic, or political—that denies the dignity of human beings made in God's image. It calls us to pledge our ultimate allegiance not to any nation, ideology, or party, but to the reign of God's righteousness made visible in Jesus Christ. To belong to this Kingdom is to embody its values by loving people through acts of mercy and acts of justice.

Jesus still calls his followers to this important work. And this means that justice is not the work of activists alone. It's the vocation of every disciple. Whether we challenge racism, support fair wages, or work for policies that protect the environment, we are taking part in Christ's ongoing work of redemption. In a culture that often equates faith with private belief, Jesus reminds us that justice is not optional; it's the public face of love.

Once we hear the call of God to love people through acts of mercy and justice, it can feel daunting. How do we begin to live this out in ordinary life? The good news is that Jesus doesn't ask us to change the world single-handedly. He invites us to take faithful steps, empowered by grace.

Practicing Mercy and Justice

When we look at the world around us, we see unimaginable suffering and injustice. Poverty, inequality, oppression, and violence are so pervasive that we hardly know where to begin. We see it in the widening gap between the rich and the poor, in families displaced by war and disaster, in communities scarred by racism and addiction, and in the silent ache of those who feel forgotten. The sheer scale of human pain can leave us feeling powerless. What difference can one person make?

Yet Scripture reminds us that God sees every wound and hears every cry. The same Spirit who stirred the prophets and strengthened the early church is still at work today, calling us not to despair but to faithfulness. When we look upon the suffering of the world through the eyes of Christ, God invites us not to turn away but to take one step closer—to become instruments of mercy and agents of justice right where we are.

Transformation begins not with grand solutions but with small, steady steps of love taken in faith. Below are a few ideas to get us thinking in the right direction. They are not intended to be a checklist but a rhythm of grace, a way of staying in sync with the heartbeat of God.

We can begin by praying differently. Instead of asking only for our own comfort or for the world's problems to simply go away, we pray for eyes to see the suffering that surrounds us and for the courage to act. This kind of prayer is dangerous because it draws us out of indifference and awakens us to compassion. It helps us notice the single mother working two jobs, the elderly neighbor who feels forgotten, and the person on the street begging for food. Prayers like this don't just change *what* we see; they change *how* we see. They open us to the Spirit's prompting, showing us where love is already at work and where we might join in the next act of mercy or justice.

We can also try to better understand the needs of the world around us and the systems that either nurture or obstruct peace and justice. Love that endures must be informed by truth, and truth is often found in the voices we are least accustomed to hearing. When we listen to the stories of those who struggle at the margins—when we allow their experiences to shape our understanding—we begin to see how mercy and justice belong together.

As we listen to the voices of those who suffer, Scripture itself begins to sound different. When we read the Bible through the eyes of the poor and the oppressed, we hear it differently—not as something used to manipulate and control, but as a word that sets people free. The cry of the prophets, the compassion of Jesus, the vision of the Kingdom—they all take on fresh urgency. This kind of learning grounds our compassion and gives direction to our action. It helps us move from good intentions to faithful participation in God's redemptive work in the world.

Next, we engage in small acts of mercy as we meet people in need. Sometimes love looks as simple as sharing a meal, visiting the sick, or sitting beside someone in grief. Mercy responds to the pain that is right in front of us; it offers presence, dignity, and hope amid suffering. Every act of mercy, no matter how small, is a means of grace through which God's love flows into the world.

God also uses these moments to help us see the deeper problems that require collective action.

This is where acts of justice come in. We speak out, vote, and act against injustice, supporting those in need despite the cost. This might look like advocating for affordable housing, working to end the death penalty, urging elected officials to defend the dignity of immigrants, or simply speaking up when silence would be easier. Acts of mercy relieve suffering; acts of justice aim at ending the conditions that cause it. Together, they reflect the fullness of God's love.

Finally, God calls us to live prophetically. This doesn't mean predicting the future or shouting on street corners; it means embodying a different way of being human. To live prophetically is to practice generosity in a culture of greed, forgiveness in a culture of vengeance, simplicity in a culture of excess, and kindness in a culture of outrage. It means bearing witness to the kingdom of God in the way we spend, speak, serve, vote, and love.

These movements—praying differently, learning faithfully, serving mercifully, acting justly, and living prophetically—are not separate callings, but one continuous rhythm of life. They are the heartbeat of Christian discipleship.

When we walk in this rhythm, even our smallest acts of faithfulness become part of God's magnificent work of renewal. Each prayer, act of compassion, and step in the pursuit of justice contributes to God's healing and restorative work in the world.

As we engage in such practices, grace doesn't just change the world; it changes us. The same love that flows through us also transforms us, awakening our hearts to the presence of Christ in all things.

Moved by Love, Transformed by Grace

Grace opens our eyes to Christ in our neighbor and moves our hands and feet in mercy and justice. That is the heart of this chapter. God does not save us *from* the world's pain so that we can look away; God saves us *for* love so we can help those who suffer and seek what is right.

I still see Jason crossing the parking lot with a sleeping bag in his arms and blisters on his feet. I wish I could say his story had a happy ending—that he found housing or recovery—but I don't know. What I do know is that in my encounter with him, Jesus showed up.

Moments like that have taught me that Christ is not confined to sanctuaries or Sunday school classrooms. We find him on street corners and in hospital waiting rooms, in shelters and rehabilitation centers—in the very places we are tempted to avoid. Grace turns those places into holy ground.

"I assure you that when you have done it for one of the least of these brothers and sisters of mine, you have done it for me" (Matthew 25:40). The church has long called such responses works of mercy and works of justice and recognized them as means of grace. Mercy meets an immediate need. Justice tries to address the deeper causes of that need. Both are love in action, and both shape us into the likeness of Christ.

So how do we live this way in our everyday lives, especially when we feel busy, pressured, and often overwhelmed by what we see? We begin with attention. We ask God for eyes to see one need today and for the courage to respond. We meet the needs we can. Then we take one step beyond the moment of mercy and ask a deeper question about cause and repair. We learn about local issues, contact an elected official, or join a ministry working for justice in our community. Small steps taken faithfully shape a life.

In these moments we are not earning favor or seeking reward. We are simply living out the grace that has already claimed us. Love flows freely because God has transformed our hearts. Over time, the dividing lines between giver and receiver begin to fade. The stranger welcomes us into a larger world. The recovering addict helps set us free. The poor reveal God's presence with a clarity we often miss.

When the church lives this way, it becomes a window into God's kingdom—a community where the poor are honored rather than pitied, where compassion deepens into friendship, and where justice is the public shape of Christian love.

Serving the poor will not fix every problem or erase every pain. But it can make God's presence real in a hurting world. It can make sure people do not suffer alone. It can take some of the suffering out of the people who are suffering. And in that shared space of mercy and justice, we experience the healing love of Christ.

This is the calling of every Christian—to be a force of love, peace, and justice in a world that God is still redeeming. And when we take even one step toward that calling, we find that Christ is already there, transforming us, transforming others, and drawing all things toward the fulfillment of God's kingdom.

CHAPTER 5

CHRISTIANS WRESTLE WITH GOD

When Faith Feels Like a Fight

When I think about faith, I often think of my grandmother. She prayed and read her Bible every day and never missed a church service. My dad once told me that when he was growing up, he never heard her say a single curse word. She was firm in her convictions, and when she thought you were doing something wrong, she didn't hesitate to let you know. In my family, my grandmother was a shining example of faith. She taught us that good Christians pray, go to church, live with honesty and modesty, and keep their language clean. If you did those things, you would do well.

But when doctors diagnosed my grandmother with Alzheimer's, that simple picture of faith began to fall apart. Although we prayed for God to heal her, or at least stop the decline, she didn't get better. She got worse.

Eventually, my parents had to move Grandma into a nursing home that could provide round-the-clock care. Over time, the disease changed her personality. The same woman who had embodied such steadfast devotion to God was now sad and angry, sometimes cursing at the nurses. With every visit, it was as if another piece of her quietly slipped away.

Near the end of her life, she pulled me close and whispered in my ear something I'll never forget: "Please kill me." There's no way to soften that memory. My grandmother's life had become a living hell. I remember driving home after a visit thinking, *God, how could you let something so bad happen to such a good woman?* It was hard for me to reconcile the God I learned about in Sunday school and the God who seemed so silent in this moment of darkness.

I didn't realize it then, but I was learning that wrestling with God isn't a sign of weak faith; it's how faith grows. What felt like losing my faith was actually the beginning of finding a deeper one.

Nevertheless, the questions were piercing. How could someone so faithful suffer so deeply? Why didn't God answer our prayers? Why would the same God she loved and served for decades allow her life to end in such anguish?

Those questions didn't just break my heart; they broke my faith. The belief system that had carried me for years no longer held. In that moment, a decision came into sharp focus: I could either walk away from my faith or wrestle with God until I found a new way to believe.

I know now that I wasn't the first or the last to feel that collapse. Sooner or later, every honest believer comes to a moment when the simple answers of childhood faith no longer hold the weight of adult pain. Faith can fracture under the pressure of suffering, but sometimes the fracture becomes the very place where grace seeps in. What looks like breaking is often the beginning of rebuilding.

In the middle of all that pain, I decided to hold onto faith and wrestle with God. I yelled at God, cried out to God, and even doubted whether God existed. But I didn't walk away. I stayed in the struggle. And somewhere in that long, painful fight, something began to change. The doubts that once threatened to undo my faith became a doorway to something deeper—a trust in God that was humbler, stronger, and more open to mystery.

That kind of faith doesn't come easily. It's hard-won, shaped through struggle and surrender; a faith that can hold both the wonder and the ache of being human. Looking back, the struggle proved to be a blessing—a blessing that reshaped not only what I believed but who I was as a follower of Jesus.

Many of us have moments when faith doesn't feel like calm assurance but more like a wrestling match with God. When prayers go unanswered. When a careful reading of Scripture raises tough questions. When grief or injustice shakes the foundations of what we thought we knew. Faith, in those seasons, isn't about feeling certain. It's about trusting in the presence and goodness of God.

Jacob's Long Night

During these times, when faith feels like a fight, we join a long line of people who have wrestled with God before us. One of the most vivid examples comes from the story of Jacob in Genesis 32. Jacob was a man who spent a lifetime trying to outwit, outrun, or outmaneuver others, only to find himself struggling with God on a dark and lonely night.

Jacob's story reaches this point after years of deceit and conflict. As a young man, he manipulated his older brother, Esau, into trading his birthright for a bowl of stew. Later, with the help of his mother, he deceived their father Isaac and stole the blessing that rightfully belonged to Esau. The betrayal tore the family apart. Esau vowed to kill him, and Jacob fled for his life, settling in a distant land, where he built a family and accumulated wealth.

But now, years later, God was calling him home, and with every step toward Esau, the tension grew, awakening memories of deceit and guilt he had long tried to bury. As he journeys back toward the brother he wronged, he's gripped by fear. Would Esau forgive him? Or would he seek revenge?

The night before their meeting, Jacob sent his family across the River Jabbok and stayed behind. Alone on the bank, the silence must have been deafening. No more deals to make. No more disguises to hide behind. Only Jacob, stripped of his status and wealth, waiting for whatever was coming next. Then suddenly, out of the darkness, someone grabbed him, and the two wrestled through the night until daybreak. Only then did Jacob realize he had been grappling not with a man, but with God.

It's a strange story—part myth, part mystery, yet fully human. Who hasn't struggled in the dark? Who hasn't struggled to make sense of fear, grief, unanswered prayer, or disappointment? Like Jacob, we come to those moments exhausted, clinging to faith by a thread, yet refusing to let go until we find a way through.

What's striking about this story is that Jacob doesn't face condemnation for his act of wrestling with God. Instead, he's blessed. In fact, the struggle itself becomes the turning point of his life.

When it ends, God gives him a new name, Israel, which means "one who struggles with God." The deceiver becomes the struggler; the schemer becomes the seeker. He leaves the encounter both limping and blessed, carrying in his body the memory of grace discovered through struggle.

Similarly, we may not wrestle beside a river, but we all have our Jabbok nights. The hospital waiting rooms where prayers go unanswered. The long nights of anxiety when we can't sleep. The grief that won't resolve. The doubts we hide because we fear what they might say about us. In those places, God often feels hidden, and keeping faith can feel like holding on to something that keeps slipping through your fingers. But it's in those nights that grace does its deepest work, shaping us through the struggle, just as it shaped Jacob.

When the night finally breaks, we don't walk away the same. The limp is important because it reminds us that transformation always comes at a cost. None of us wrestles with God and walks away unchanged. Real faith leaves a mark. Yet that mark is not a sign of weakness; it's the trace of grace left by an encounter that makes us new. Jacob's limp was not punishment; it was evidence that he had been in the transforming presence of God.

Similarly, when we wrestle honestly with our faith—when we bring our doubts, anger, and confusion into conversation with God—we, too, walk away changed. We may not leave with all our questions answered, but we often find something deeper: a sense of peace that doesn't depend on exhaustive explanations, a trust that grows through struggle, and a humility that keeps us open to mystery and grace.

Jacob's story offers a glimpse into what faithful struggle looks like. It reminds us that wrestling with God is not evidence of faltering faith but the very process by which faith matures.

Jacob's long night is our long night too. His story isn't just ancient history; it's a mirror of our own experience. Every believer knows what it's like to wrestle in prayer, to struggle with doubt, or to face suffering that defies explanation. Like Jacob, we discover that faith often grows strongest in the dark, when we keep holding on to God even though nothing makes sense.

Wrestling as a Practice of Faith

Most of us at some point find ourselves wrestling—with God, with Scripture, with suffering, with ourselves. Faith that is alive will, sooner or later, lead to some kind of struggle.

The mistake we often make is thinking that struggle signals failure. We assume that strong faith means belief without questions, devotion without doubt. But the opposite is true. Struggle is the proving ground of faith. Just as muscles grow through resistance, faith deepens through the tension of wrestling with God.

A few years ago, I injured my back. I hadn't been exercising much, but when good waves came to Cocoa Beach, I surfed long sessions several days in a row. The muscles that supported my lower back had weakened from inactivity, and all that paddling and popping up pushed them past their limit.

The pain hit suddenly—as if lightning shot through my spine—and I collapsed to the floor. An MRI showed that I had several bulging discs pressing on a nerve. The doctors wanted to operate, but I decided to try physical therapy first.

That decision led me to a therapist named Curtis, who helped me recover without surgery. Every other day for six weeks, I pushed through exercises that stretched my muscles, strengthened them, and often left them burning with fatigue. Some days I could barely finish, but Curtis reminded me that the struggle was part of the healing. The resistance, he said, was what made me stronger. He was right. Every press, every ache, every stretch was part of the recovery. The only way to rebuild strength was to embrace the discomfort and trust that it had a purpose.

Faith grows the same way. The struggles that bear down on us—the griefs, the setbacks, the doubts—become the means through which God restores and strengthens us. Grace becomes the therapy that heals what's been torn.

During my last visit, Curtis warned me that if I stopped doing the exercises, I'd end up back in therapy. I asked, "How long do I have to keep doing them?"

He smiled and said, "For the rest of your life." Faith works like that too. The wrestling never ends. It's not a single breakthrough but a lifelong practice of staying open to grace and trusting that every struggle can make us stronger.

The practices we explored in earlier chapters—surrendering, forgiving, exercising empathy, serving with mercy and justice—invite transformation. But transformation isn't easy or predictable. As we practice our faith and reflect on what we experience, we often discover that our old beliefs can't bear the weight of new realities. Something must stretch, bend, or even break before it can be made new.

I've seen this in my own ministry. I've sat beside hospital beds where faith looked more like silence than song, where people didn't have the strength to pray but still wanted someone to hold their hand and pray for them. I know people who didn't walk away from God but from the church, because when they honestly shared their doubts, they stopped feeling like they belonged. And I've felt it myself, waking up some days and thinking, *Do I really believe all this stuff?*

Times like these remind me that grace does its deepest work during seasons of struggle and doubt, when we bring what we believe about God into conversation with what God is teaching us in and through our lived experience. Transformation happens in the tension between the beliefs we once held with confidence and what we're learning as we continue to name our pain, ask tough questions, and listen for God's voice in the discomfort. This is where we find a faith that can hold both mystery and meaning.

Again, this kind of wrestling doesn't weaken our faith; it strengthens it. It keeps faith alive and growing, dynamic and real. Without it, our beliefs can harden into certainty, and certainty can quietly turn into idolatry—when we begin trusting our own *ideas* about God more than we actually trust *God*. Still, when we stay engaged in the struggle, God uses it as a means of grace, a practice through which the Holy Spirit transforms us into the image of Christ.

As with the other practices in this book, wrestling with God isn't meant to happen in isolation. The Christian life is a communal journey, not a solo climb. We need others who can help us hold on when our grip weakens, friends who remind us of grace when we can't feel it ourselves. We need healthy churches and small groups that make room for honest questions and stories of brokenness.

Sadly, many people have experienced the opposite. Religious leaders have communicated that their doubts are dangerous, their struggles are shameful, and their acceptance depends on blind obedience to authority. But true Christian community isn't built on uniformity; it's built on love. When we're honest about our struggles and our Christian friends listen with empathy, something holy happens. The love between us becomes a channel of grace, a source of strength that steadies us until we can stand again on our own.

This shows us that wrestling with God isn't about fighting against faith; it's about staying in relationship. It's about trusting that God can handle our hardest questions and will meet us in our deepest struggles. It's about staying connected to one another when life feels like it's falling apart, believing that God works through our friends to strengthen us for the journey. To wrestle with faith is to keep showing up in prayer, in worship, and in community, even when faith feels uncertain.

Doubt Is Not the Enemy

If wrestling with God is a means of grace, then doubt isn't something to fear—it's something to face with honesty and courage. As explained previously, doubt is often the doorway to a deeper, more resilient kind of faith.

Unfortunately, many Christians learn to see doubt as a problem to fix or a sin to confess. We're told that "real faith" never wavers, that strong believers never question God. But more often than not, the opposite is true. Faith without doubt isn't really faith; it's certainty. And certainty leaves no room for trust. In contrast, true faith makes room for doubt, acknowledging that God is greater than our understanding and that there will always be more to discover than what we think we know.

This means that when we acknowledge our uncertainty before God, we're not betraying faith; *we're exercising faith*. We're saying, "God, I don't understand, but I still trust in your goodness and want to be in relationship with you." Here we see that honest doubt is an opening, not a rupture. It's a sign that faith is still alive and growing.

We see this truth played out in Scripture. Some of the most faithful people in the Bible wrestled with doubt. Abraham argued with God about justice (Genesis 18:23-25). Moses doubted God's calling to lead the Israelites out of slavery (Exodus 3:11). Job demanded answers from the depths of his suffering (Job 13:23-24). Even Jesus cried out from the cross, "My God, my God, why have you forsaken me?" (Mark 15:34 NRSVue). These moments don't expose weakened faith; they reveal a faith that is strong, authentic, and engaged.

So if doubt isn't the opposite of faith, what is? It's fear that hardens into the kind of distrust that keeps us silent and stagnant, afraid to ask questions or admit uncertainty. When fear takes hold, it doesn't just stifle our curiosity, it begins to erode our trust. Instead of waiting on God, we start relying on ourselves. Instead of listening for God's voice, we fill the silence with our own answers. And once we stop trusting, disobedience follows.

We turn away and do what seems right in our own eyes rather than what God is calling us to do.

But true faith is different. It leans in where fear pulls away. It waits and listens where fear tries to take control. Unlike fearful distrust, faith keeps us open to God's transforming presence. Even when we don't understand, it empowers us to pray, "I believe; help my unbelief!" (Mark 9:24 NRSVue).

When we create space in our faith communities for honest doubt, we make room for real growth. We invite people out of hiding and into an authentic relationship with God and one another. We begin to understand that doubt, when met with grace, doesn't destroy faith but helps it mature.

In the end, doubt isn't a detour from faith. It's part of the journey. It humbles us, deepens our compassion, and teaches us to rely not on our own understanding but on the living presence of God who walks with us, even in the darkness.

If doubt can deepen faith, certainty can just as easily distort it. Where doubt opens us to grace, certainty closes us off from it.

The Sin of Certainty

When we cling too tightly to our own understanding, faith stops growing. It becomes smaller, more rigid, more afraid. What begins as confidence in God can quietly turn into confidence in ourselves—our interpretations of the Bible, our rituals and traditions, our need to be right. That's when faith ceases to be trust and turns into a compulsion to control.

Contemporary biblical scholar Peter Enns calls this "the sin of certainty," reminding us that our obsession with being right is, at its core, a spiritual problem.[1] When we demand absolute answers from God and treat our beliefs as infallible, we stop letting them be shaped by the living God they're meant to reveal. Instead of remaining open and receptive, we become defensive and closed. We feel compelled to protect and preach our convictions at all costs (even at the cost of our most important relationships). Over time, our posture toward God shifts from trust to control, and we begin to worship our theology rather than the triune God to which our theology points.

Throughout Scripture, God repeatedly confronts this impulse. In the wilderness, the Israelites longed for the security of Egypt as they faced the uncertainty of following God into freedom (Exodus 16:2-3). Some Pharisees in Jesus's day clung to the safety of their strict interpretations of Scripture instead of embracing the risky, relational grace Jesus offered to all (Matthew 23:23-24). Even the disciples struggled to understand that Jesus's kingdom could not be controlled or contained by human expectations (Acts 1:6-7).

Whenever people trade trust for certainty, the result is the same: Hearts close, ears stop listening, and faith becomes more about self-protection than the vulnerable trust that keeps us open to God.

You don't have to look far to see how this plays out today. Just turn on the news or scroll through social media. The loudest voices usually get the most attention, the ones that attack, argue, or act with the most bravado. We see it in politics, where winning the argument matters more than solving the problem, and in churches, where people sometimes care more about being right than being like Christ. Faith can easily turn into a performance, about who sounds the most certain, the most "biblical," or the most "strong." Yet when faith becomes about proving a point instead of following Jesus, it loses the humility that makes it holy.

Certainty may feel safe, but it tends to isolate us. It leaves little room for humility, learning, or growth. It breeds judgment toward those who see differently and anxiety toward anything we can't explain. Over time, certainty doesn't just close hearts; it makes religion authoritarian, convincing people that faith is less about trusting God and more about blind obedience to religious (and political) authority. In our very efforts to protect faith, we end up corrupting it into its opposite. Sometimes the Bible reminds us that real faith is not about having infallible truth but trusting in the God who is *the* Truth and allowing the Holy Spirit to draw us ever deeper into the mystery of divine grace. It doesn't hide its own limitations and remembers that God is always bigger than our ideas about God.

When I was teaching philosophy at Florida Southern College, I had a student who was struggling deeply with his faith. He had grown up in a church that taught that true Christians must take the Bible literally and that science was an enemy of God's truth. The private K–12 Christian school he attended reinforced those ideas. When he was living in that world, his faith felt secure. But when he began taking college classes, many of his beliefs were turned upside down.

In these classes, he met professors who were simply trying to understand how the world works: asking questions, conducting experiments, and following the evidence wherever it led. He was surprised that these scientists didn't look down on him for being a

Christian, nor did they try to steal his faith. In fact, the more they encouraged his curiosity, the more he learned—and the harder it became to keep believing the same way. When he went home on breaks and tried to talk with his parents and pastor about his questions, they quickly shut him down. "Those professors are teaching you lies," they said. "You just need to believe God's word."

Knowing that I was not only a professor but also a pastor, he eventually came to see me after class. He was torn between what he was learning and what others had insisted he believe. After considering his options, he was convinced that he needed to give up his faith altogether. We talked for a long time, and I told him that the version of Christianity he grew up with was not the only one. Other Christian traditions view science not as a threat to faith but as another way to explore truth. I also reminded him that many of history's greatest scientists were people of deep faith, convinced that studying the natural world was an important way of loving God with their minds.

After our conversation, he began meeting with the college chaplain, joined a small group, and started taking religion classes that changed how he saw the Bible. Over time, his faith was reborn not as certainty but as trust. He came to believe that God was not in conflict with science but present in all truth and discovery. Through this process, he developed a faith of his own, one that allowed more room for mystery. But it required him to admit that God is bigger than any of his own ideas about God.

This is what maturing faith looks like. It's not built on having all the answers but on remaining open to the Spirit who leads us into new ways of seeing and believing. Jesus said, "When the

Spirit of Truth comes, he will guide you in all truth" (John 16:13). Notice the movement—*guide you in* all truth, not simply drop it in your lap. Truth in the life of faith is about a growing relationship with God, not a set of religious teachings that we seize and master.

The sin of certainty isn't about believing too much; it's about believing we've already figured everything out and feeling compelled to convince everyone else that we're right. When we surrender that illusion, we discover that true faith is not about knowing everything but about trusting in the goodness of God even when we don't have all the answers. It's a faith that listens, learns, and leans on God's presence rather than its own understanding:

Trust in the LORD with all your heart;
don't rely on your own intelligence.
Know him in all your paths,
and he will keep your ways straight.
(Proverbs 3:5-6)

Holding On Until Daybreak: The Blessing in the Wrestling

When we let go of the need for control and stay in the struggle, we discover that God meets us there. The wrestling itself becomes a source of blessing, a sacred encounter that changes us from the inside out.

That's what happened to Jacob. When the long night ended, he wasn't the same man who started the fight. He limped away from the river, wounded yet blessed. His limp wasn't a sign of failure; it was a symbol of transformation. The one who once schemed and grasped now walks with humility and reliance on God. He no longer demands God's blessing on his terms but receives it as a gift.

Every real encounter with God leaves a mark. But it's not a mark of defeat. It's the imprint of grace. The pain that once felt like punishment becomes evidence of God's presence. What once broke us opens the door for healing and restoration.

And that blessing isn't just for Jacob. It belongs to everyone who has wrestled through a long night of loss or doubt, questioning whether faith is still possible. Jacob's story reminds us that we don't have to hide from those moments. God isn't threatened by our questions, anger, or fear. God meets us in the struggle and stays with us long after we run out of strength.

This is the mystery of grace: blessing often comes disguised as struggle. It's rarely comfortable and never predictable, but it's real. The struggle loosens our grip on control and teaches us to rely on God's sustaining presence. It humbles us, softens us, and opens our hearts to others who also wrestle. The limp becomes a quiet reminder that none of us walk this journey untouched.

Wrestling with God isn't a sign of weak faith. It's living faith. It's the faith of those who keep praying even when answers are delayed, who continue loving even when love is costly, who keep trusting even when understanding is hard to find. The blessing isn't in certainty or victory but in relationship—in refusing to let go because we've learned that God never lets go of us.

Jacob's long night becomes our invitation. We all experience seasons when faith feels like holding on for dear life. But the night isn't endless. There's always a dawn on the horizon. Holding on until daybreak isn't about winning the struggle or solving the mystery. It's about maintaining relationship and trusting that the God who meets us in darkness will lead us into new life.

Faith isn't a straight line from doubt to certainty or from weakness to strength. It's a steady movement toward deeper trust in a God who refuses to let go. If we pay attention, we see that all the practices in this book lead us here. Each one leads us to moments where belief is tested by experience, and control must give way to grace. Wrestling with God isn't a detour from the life of faith. It's one of the main ways God shapes us into Christ's image. It's what keeps faith alive.

A faith that refuses to wrestle is a faith that never grows. It stays small, safe, and manageable. But a faith that dares to question, to weep, to wait is a faith that matures into love. It's the kind that can hold both knowing and unknowing, joy and sorrow, hope and lament. It's the kind that can rejoice with those who rejoice and weep with those who weep.

Maybe that's what it really means to be blessed—not that life is easy or that prayers are always answered, but that God is present in the struggle itself. Present in the questions, the tears, the silence, and the surrender. The blessing isn't in escaping the fight; it's in discovering that we are never alone in it.

So if you find yourself wrestling, take heart. It doesn't mean your faith is failing; it means it's alive. It means that you are loving God with everything you are and everything you have—questions and all. Keep showing up. Keep praying. Keep asking your questions and telling God the truth about what you feel. Trust that somewhere in the dark, God is holding on to you too.

And when the dawn finally comes, you may find that the blessing you were looking for wasn't an answer to a problem, but the presence of God in your pain—the same presence that has been there all along, wrestling with you, carrying you, and leading you toward a faith that is humbler, stronger, and more full of grace.

CHAPTER 6

CHRISTIANS SHARE FAITH

I was a rambunctious and sometimes rebellious kid. My parents took me to church every Sunday for Sunday school and worship. On Sunday nights, we returned for youth Bible study and then another "salvation service" focused on evangelism. We even went to church on Wednesday nights for in-depth Bible study. I often joke that one reason I became United Methodist was so I wouldn't have to go to church quite so much!

From all those hours invested, I received many gifts. I learned the basics of the Christian faith: that God created the world good, that human beings turned from God in sin, and that God sent Jesus to save us. I learned that I could receive Jesus, be forgiven of my sins, and live in a way that pleases God and helps others. I discovered that the power of the Holy Spirit works to reshape me into the image of Christ and that I can trust God in life, in death, and life beyond death. I learned to treasure the Bible as God's word, memorizing verses that would later sustain me. And I learned that God cares deeply for the poor and calls us to show love to the outcast and vulnerable. This foundation gave me what I needed to wrestle with God and discover my own faith as an adult.

But even with all this teaching, what marked me most deeply was not a sermon or a class—it was my grandmother's faith lived out in love.

As I mentioned in the previous chapter, my grandmother was a devout Christian woman, and I truly felt that she adored me. She was one of the few people in my life to whom I really listened when she talked about God—not because she was ordained or had advanced training but because I knew that she loved me unconditionally.

One day, she pulled me aside, looked me in the eyes, and said with deep sincerity, "Mark, God has a special plan for your life." I don't believe she ever spoke those words to her other grandchildren. For me, they were like impressions in wet cement, shaping me far longer than she could have imagined.

Even in the years when I drifted into destructive choices, I could not escape those words. Looking back, I know they are one of the reasons I decided to dedicate my life to Christian service. Her words also left me wondering, What makes faith stick? What really shapes a child's faith for a lifetime?

Maybe you have someone like that in your own story. A grandmother or grandfather, a parent, or maybe even a neighbor or Sunday school teacher whose faith was real to you not because they were perfect but because you could feel their love and see their trust in God. Take a moment to remember them.

This experience with my grandmother taught me an important lesson when I became a parent: The greatest predictor of your child's lifelong faith is not how often you take them to church or how eloquently you defend your beliefs. It's you—and the way you live when no one else is watching.

Modeling Faith

Scripture names this same reality in Timothy's story. The author of the Second Letter to Timothy writes: "I am reminded of your sincere faith, which first lived in your grandmother Lois and your mother Eunice. I'm sure that this faith is also inside you" (2 Timothy 1:5).

What Timothy witnessed in his mother and grandmother was not mere belief but a genuine trust in God that showed itself in daily life. The author suggests that faith is passed on not primarily through indoctrination but through the lived example of trusted people whose lives make the gospel believable.

Notice the emphasis here on *lived* faith. The author of the letter doesn't say that Lois and Eunice simply instructed Timothy about God; he says faith *lived* in them. Their faith wasn't reserved for Sundays but shaped their pattern of life every day of the week. In watching them pray, forgive, endure hardship, and hold fast to hope, Timothy caught a vision of what authentic trust in God looks like. What the author noticed in Timothy's family is exactly what our kids need from us today—not a perfect belief system but a living, breathing example of what faith looks like in everyday life. Timothy didn't just hear about faith; he watched it come alive right before his own eyes.

This is a great model for parents, grandparents, and mentors today. While it's important to teach our children the core beliefs of the faith, research confirms what the writer of the letter already sensed: Kids are far more likely to embrace faith when they see it lived out in the people they love and trust most. It's not long lectures or academic Bible lessons that make the biggest difference; it's watching the people who care for them, especially their parents, pray, forgive, serve, and treat others with kindness. They notice the small things, too—how we treat a server at a restaurant or whether we speak patiently when frustrated. These little moments preach louder than we realize. Children pick up what faith looks like by observing it in real life. When our words and our actions line up, when they see us lean on God in both joy and hardship, they begin to believe that the gospel is real.

So what does modeling look like in real life?

Most obviously, we pass on faith through the spiritual practices that shape our days. In addition to the practices we've explored in this book, this also includes praying over meals, at bedtime, or before a trip; reading Scripture; listening to Christian music; spending time with other believers; and joyfully joining in the life of the church. These habits may feel small, but over time they become the rhythms our children remember. What we make room for in our schedules shows what really matters to us. And when our kids see that discipleship practices are not optional extras but are woven naturally into family life, they begin to recognize that faith is more than words or ideas; it's a way of life.

We also model faith when we practice humility, wrestle with God, and take responsibility for our mistakes. Children quickly notice when our actions don't match our words, which is why integrity matters so much. When they hear us say, "I'm sorry I lost my temper. I know God wants me to be more patient," and then see us try to do better next time, it teaches them two things at once: Honesty and accountability are important aspects of faith, and following Jesus is about growing in love, not achieving perfection.

Like Lois and Eunice, every time we model faith in these ways, we show our children what a life with God looks like in practice. They are watching our actions more than they are listening to our words, quietly learning from the choices we make and the priorities we set. As they get older and decide for themselves how to live, they will remember the patterns of trust, love, and hope they first witnessed in us.

Modeling our faith in these ways can feel overwhelming. And if you're anything like me, you often fall short. Parents today face challenges Lois and Eunice never imagined: families stretched by demanding schedules, screens that dominate our attention, a consumer culture that equates worth with possessions and achievements, and political divisions that fracture both families and congregations. Many parents feel inadequate, unprepared, or simply exhausted. Life's pressures and personal struggles can keep us from modeling Jesus as consistently as we would like.

But remember, God does not expect perfection but works through ordinary acts of faithfulness. Furthermore, we are not asked to carry this responsibility alone. When children are baptized, they are welcomed into the family of God. This means that all the kids in the church are our kids, whether we have biological children or not.

This is more than a sentimental idea; it's a covenant we make with God. At baptism, parents are asked: "Will you nurture these children in Christ's holy Church, that by your teaching and example they may be guided to accept God's grace for themselves, to profess their faith openly, and to lead a Christian life?" Parents answer: "I will." In this way, they are promising not just to bring their child to church or teach a list of doctrines but to model and teach the faith in their daily lives.

Also, notice that responsibility does not end with parents. The pastor then turns to the whole congregation and asks: "Will you nurture one another in the Christian faith and life and include these persons now before you in your care?" And the people respond together: "With God's help we will proclaim the good news and live according to the example of Christ. We will surround these persons with a community of love and forgiveness, that they may grow in their service to others. We will pray for them, that they may be true disciples who walk in the way that leads to life."[1] Here, the congregation promises to model their faith in how they live their lives and love the child being baptized.

These are not mere words—they are covenant promises. Every time a child is baptized, the entire church assumes a sacred responsibility to model Christ and nurture the child's faith. Their spiritual growth is not just the parents' responsibility but the shared calling of the entire body of Christ.

Imagine what it would look like if the whole church truly embraced every child as "our kids." No child would ever feel like they were walking through life alone. They would grow up surrounded by people who know their names, celebrate their milestones, and pray for them with genuine love. Children would see faith modeled not just by their parents but by dozens of other adults—mentors, teachers, choir members, ushers, and volunteers—who reflect Christ's love in different ways. Teenagers wrestling with questions would know there are safe places and trusted adults they can turn to for honest conversation. Young adults heading off to college would know they have a church family back home, a group of people praying for them, cheering for them, and waiting to welcome them whenever they return. And parents would feel the strength of a whole community standing with them, reminding them they don't have to raise faithful children alone. That's what the family of God is meant to look like—a community where every child belongs, every parent is supported, and every generation is nurtured in faith.

Together, as families and as a church community, we share the joyful work of nurturing faith and raising the next generation to follow Christ.

It truly takes a village to raise a follower of Jesus. We need other Christians to model their faith and pour it into our kids when they are not at home. We need children's ministers who help our kids learn faithfulness by turning to God in prayer. Youth pastors who teach teenagers how to handle bullies without violence. Volunteers who show patience and love as our kids experiment with different identities.

I've seen this kind of impact firsthand. Years ago, there was an elementary school student in our church who struggled deeply with insecurity and often felt invisible at school. The children's minister made a point of greeting her by name every Sunday, asking about her week, and encouraging her to share in class. It seemed like such a small act, but over time it changed the way this young girl saw herself. She began to participate more and looked forward to coming to church. The simple kindness and encouragement of that leader helped her understand that her life mattered to God.

That's the power of a church family. When adults outside the home invest in children and teenagers, their faith is reinforced, and their sense of belonging grows. Parents can't do it alone, and God never intended them to. The whole church plays a role in raising the next generation.

God calls every member of the body of Christ to stand in the gap and reinforce the habits of faith that parents are trying to develop at home. When children see devotion not only lived out by parents and grandparents but also by pastors, teachers, and mentors, they learn that following Jesus isn't just a family tradition—it's a lifelong journey with all God's people.

Teaching Faith

All of this shows that faith is often first *caught* through our example. But faith that is caught only matures when it is also *taught*. Just as parents, grandparents, and church members model faith, we are also called to offer teachings that help it take root. Paul reminds Timothy of this when he writes: "Since childhood you have known the holy scriptures that help you to be wise in a way that leads to salvation through faith that is in Christ Jesus" (2 Timothy 3:15). Timothy didn't just have good role models—his mother and grandmother also took time to teach him the story of Jesus and how to read and understand the Scriptures. Their example and instruction worked together to form a faith that would sustain him for life.

Teaching our kids about Jesus and helping them engage with the Bible can feel overwhelming, even as it stretches our own faith. But you don't need a seminary degree to share what you believe. What matters most is approaching the task with humility and honesty, inviting open conversation rather than trying to have all the answers. Reading Bible stories together, showing them how you pray, and guiding them into the rhythms of worship are important, but so is creating space for questions and even doubts.

I remember when my boys were little, we began saying a simple prayer at dinner, the same one I had learned as a child: "God is great, God is good, let us thank him for our food. By his hands we all are fed, give us, O Lord, our daily bread." At first, the words were just sounds they tried to copy. But over time, they learned the rhythm, then the meaning, and eventually the prayer became their own. Even now, as teenagers and young adults, that prayer is still part of our family table. It reminds me that the simplest practices, repeated with love, often leave the deepest and most lasting impressions.

I also remember my kids asking many questions, and even though I didn't always have the answers, I encouraged curiosity and critical thinking. This is what gives children permission to wrestle with God and develop a faith that is truly their own. I wanted them to know the difference between blind submission to religious authority and learning to love and trust God.

When children receive authoritarian answers, it can shut down their questions, make them feel unheard, and eventually push them away from faith altogether. It also makes it difficult for them to develop a faith of their own, because this requires a safe and open place to wrestle with difficult questions and experiences. But when we create space for honest wondering, they discover that God can handle their questions—and so can we.

What about you? How are you gently encouraging the children in your life to wonder, to question, and to discover a faith that feels real to them?

I've met parents who never talk about faith because they just aren't comfortable doing so. Sometimes they feel inadequate, worried they don't know enough. Others carry bad experiences from their own upbringing and don't want to repeat old patterns. Still others fear that pushing too hard might backfire and drive their kids away. While all of this is understandable, the result is often silence that leaves kids without tools to draw on when life gets hard. In contrast, I've also seen parents who gently weave Scripture into conversations—quoting a verse when a child feels anxious or praying together before a big test. Those small acts give kids a framework for making sense of life and a foundation to return to when they face doubts or struggles. This, too, is part of what it means for Christians to share faith with the next generation: to give instruction on our basic beliefs and spiritual practices. If our faith doesn't make it beyond the walls of the church, it risks becoming little more than Sunday words rather than a lived reality.

Some parents who are suspicious of organized religion say, "I'm not opposed to faith; I just want my kids to decide for themselves." That's also understandable. It reflects a desire to give children freedom and avoid pressuring them. But how can kids decide for themselves when the options aren't clearly laid out? If we don't talk about faith in the home, our kids will by default absorb a secular path that can eclipse Christianity as a real option. Furthermore, research shows that faith rarely grows on its own. The strongest influence on a child's spirituality is not friends, culture, or even a youth group but the example and teaching of parents.[2] When children grow up with guidance in spiritual practices, Scripture, prayer, and honest conversations, they have something to work with as they make their own decisions about religion.

Teaching faith isn't about forcing conformity or demanding that children think and act exactly like us. Rather, it's a gift. When we teach the faith, we give kids tools for their own spiritual journeys. Introducing them to Scripture, prayer, worship, and other time-tested practices doesn't limit them. Even if they never become Christians, it can still equip them to face life with wisdom and resilience. Like handing someone a compass before a long journey, we're not dictating every step of the path; we're providing guidance to help them navigate the doubts, suffering, and moral decisions they will inevitably face.

Think about what happens if you set out on a long hike without a compass or a map. At first, the path may seem clear, and you can get by just following your instincts. But sooner or later, the trail splits or you hit rough terrain, and without any sense of direction, it's easy to wander aimlessly or even get lost. In the same way, when kids step into the world without any spiritual guidance, they may do fine for a while. But when suffering comes, or when they face moral crossroads, they lack the bearings to know which way to turn. Teaching them faith won't keep them from struggling, but it gives them a true north to find their way when life feels uncertain.

This is why Christians should both model and teach faith. Only then do our children gain both the compass they need and instructions on how to use it.

And remember, we don't do this work alone. God designed the family and the church to partner together in raising the next generation. As parents, you can lean on your church family when you run out of resources or feel like you've reached the limit of your own knowledge and experience. Sunday school, youth groups, confirmation classes, and mentoring relationships are meant to reinforce and expand what is taught at home.

When churches are limited in these areas—whether because of a lack of resources or such a small number of kids that it's difficult to build a robust children's and youth ministry—they can partner with other congregations in their area. As I write this book, the church I currently serve is underresourced in youth ministry. While we are working on a plan to hire a youth minister and build a comprehensive program for our teens, we've had to reach out to another United Methodist church in our area for curriculum recommendations, confirmation classes, and fun outings. We've also leaned on denominational resources like the Warren W. Willis Camp and Conference Center and the Wesley Foundation college ministries. In addition, pastors can directly support parents by sharing good books, articles, podcasts, and learning opportunities that help deepen understanding and build confidence. In this way, the responsibility of passing on faith is never carried by parents alone. It is a shared calling, rooted in the promise that God works through both family and community to form children in Christ.

Isolation vs. Formation

As should be clear, what I am describing is quite different from certain fundamentalist approaches that equate passing faith to children with cultural isolation. Parents may remove their kids from public schools, keep them away from sports teams, or forbid friendships with anyone outside their church community. Entertainment, books, and even conversations are carefully controlled out of fear that outside voices will corrupt their children's faith. Instead of preparing kids to live in a world of diverse people and ideas, this approach attempts to shield them from it entirely. The desire to protect is understandable, but when fear is the main motivator, children rarely learn how to engage culture faithfully when they grow up.

When parents confuse isolation with formation, they treat the world as something to hide from rather than a place where Christ calls us to bear witness. The result is often a fragile faith, unprepared for the complexity of life in a pluralistic culture. At times, it can even harden into judgmentalism, producing Christians who are quick to condemn but slow to love.

I've seen the effects of this firsthand in pastoral ministry. One young adult I knew grew up in a home where every outside influence was treated as a threat. His parents monitored every friendship, threw away all his popular music, and discouraged questions. For a while, it seemed like the strategy worked—he usually followed the rules, stayed out of trouble, and knew all the right answers in youth group. But when he left for college, he felt unprepared to navigate new ideas and relationships. With no tools to engage differences, his faith crumbled under the pressure. He cut himself off from the church and started rebelling in ways that shocked his parents.

I think of another young adult who grew up differently. Her parents taught her Scripture and prayer at home but also encouraged her to ask questions, make friends with people of other beliefs, and get involved in the world around her. She learned to interpret culture through the lens of the gospel rather than avoid it altogether. By the time she left home, her faith had been tested and stretched in healthy ways. Today, she is thriving as a thoughtful, engaged Christian who carries her faith into every corner of life.

What our children need is not a bubble to hide in, but a model of how to live with grace and courage in a complicated world. They need to see us respond to differences with love so they can learn to do the same. If we retreat from the world, our children miss the chance to watch us engage people who are different with grace and Christlike compassion. That's how kids learn: by watching us live our faith in the real world.

Jesus himself prayed to God:

> *I'm not asking that you take them out of this world but that you keep them safe from the evil one. They don't belong to this world, just as I don't belong to this world. Make them holy in the truth; your word is truth. As you sent me into the world, so I have sent them into the world.*
>
> *(John 17:15-18)*

Notice what he does not pray for. He does not ask that his followers be removed from tension, conflict, or the complexities of ordinary life. Instead, he asks that they be protected and sent. To say that we do not belong to the world doesn't mean we should be disengaged or withdrawn. It means our identity is not defined by the world's values, even though our lives remain deeply rooted in its realities. Jesus doesn't form a people who escape the world; he forms a people who live differently within it. They stay present—in workplaces, neighborhoods, friendships, and public life—but their loyalty is anchored elsewhere. Their posture is shaped not by fear or control but by love.

So instead of fear-based isolation, we nurture resilient faith in the real world. We raise children not to hide from culture but to enter it with courage, compassion, and conviction. And this matters because the practices we live out in daily life slowly shape who our children are becoming. When we admit our mistakes and ask forgiveness from someone we've hurt, we are teaching them humility and empathy. When we involve them in serving meals at a food pantry or collecting supplies for neighbors in need, we are forming compassion and generosity. When they see us pray in both joyful and difficult moments, they learn that faith can carry them through life's ups and downs. These simple practices are not just family traditions. They are the training ground where God nurtures a trusting and loving faith that lasts a lifetime.

The Impression We Leave

Who first modeled faith for you? Who left their fingerprints in the wet cement of your life? Maybe it was a parent or grandparent, an aunt or uncle, a brother or sister. Or maybe it was someone outside your family. Like family members, mentors, coaches, and teachers can leave lasting impressions that shape our faith in powerful ways.

When I entered my junior year of college, I was a fiery young man—passionate about my faith, but also argumentative and defensive. After becoming a father at nineteen, I returned to the church and changed my major from graphic design to religion. One of my first classes was Basic Christian Beliefs with a professor named Waite Willis. His lectures and reading assignments challenged everything I thought I already knew, and I often reacted with anxiety and anger. I argued with him in class and then followed him to his office to argue some more.

It would have been easy for Dr. Willis to dismiss me as exhausting or unreachable, but he never did. He treated me with kindness and respect, welcoming me into his office again and again. What he didn't know early on was that beneath all my defensiveness, I was in deep personal pain—navigating young fatherhood, a fragile marriage, and the stress of working full-time to support a family. His willingness to listen opened the door for me to start sharing my struggles.

One day, sitting in his office, something shifted. I don't remember the details of our conversation, but as he spoke, I was struck by the compassion in his eyes. In that moment, I had the thought: *He loves you. He is not trying to take your faith away but to help you find a faith of your own.* Looking back, I think that was the still small voice of God pointing me in a new direction.

That encounter changed me. Through Dr. Willis's genuine concern and thorough teaching, my heart started to open, and so did my mind. Looking back, I can see the sequence clearly. First, his consistent kindness built trust, and that trust opened my heart. Only then was I able to open my mind to new ideas, new possibilities, and a broader view of faith. That's often how it works: Love opens the door for truth to come in.

In this way, Dr. Willis was doing for me what Lois and Eunice had once done for Timothy and what my parents and grandparents had once done for me. They each lived a sincere, authentic faith that made the gospel believable—not by force or argument but through love that built trust. Just as my grandmother's simple words left an impression in the wet cement of my young heart, Dr. Willis's Christlike love left an impression during a critical season of my adult life. Again, faith is not just taught but caught, and that takes root when we see it embodied in people we trust.

In my conversations with Dr. Willis I discovered that Christianity was bigger than what I experienced in the small church of my childhood. Slowly, I developed a faith shaped by the breadth of the Christian tradition and the grace of God who met me through a professor's patience and love. I discovered a way of believing that connected with my own experience and has carried me through the years. Dr. Willis also identified my gifts and encouraged me to attend seminary, which began my journey toward ordained ministry. He's a wonderful example of someone who modeled and taught faith in a way that leaves a permanent mark on one's life. He did it for me and, I'm sure, many others throughout his career.

That's the power of passing on your faith. You never know when something you say or do will leave a mark that leaves a lasting impression. Again, who was that person for you? If someone comes to mind, pause and give thanks for them.

It is also important to pause and ask, What impression am I leaving on others, especially the kids and young adults in my life? Every one of us is shaping the people around us, whether we realize it or not. Our attitudes, our words, our priorities, and the way we handle both joy and hardship leave a mark. Children will forget specific sermons or teachings, but they rarely forget how we treated them, how we treated others, and whether our faith was real in daily life.

Think for a moment about the quiet, ordinary moments that make the biggest difference: how you respond when you've made a mistake, how you talk about people who frustrate you, how you serve those in need. These impressions are like seeds scattered in the soil of a young heart. Some will take root immediately, while others may remain dormant for years until a crisis or a turning point in life awakens them.

As parents, grandparents, or mentors, we can't control every outcome, but we can be intentional about the example we set. If the pattern of our lives communicates love for God and love for others, then even when our kids wander or wrestle with doubt, they will have a living memory of what genuine faith looks like. That memory can become a guidepost for them, just as Lois and Eunice's faith became a guidepost for Timothy.

So ask yourself, when your children or grandchildren look back years from now, what will they remember about the way you lived your faith?

The practice we focused on in this chapter is simple but important: Christians share faith with the next generation. We weave the love of Christ into ordinary family life. We teach Scripture and prayer. We model integrity and forgiveness. We join the church in raising children not in fear but in grace.

One day, may our children look back and say, "I saw how they lived—and that's why I believe." That is what it means for Christians to share their faith with the next generation, to pass on a living legacy of trust in Christ.

Putting Love First

The practices in this chapter are not a magic formula. They do not guarantee that your children will adopt your faith, whether your particular expression of it or Christianity at all. Faith cannot be forced or achieved through perfect parenting.

Many faithful parents pray, model, teach, and love with deep sincerity, only to see their children drift away during their teenage or adult years. Some show little interest, while others reject organized religion entirely. I personally understand the pain of that reality. When a child chooses a different path, it can feel like a loss. And loss brings grief.

Part of mature faith is learning to accept what we cannot control. Our children are not extensions of us. They are not projects to complete. They are individuals—created in God's image, entrusted to our care for a season, and ultimately responsible for their own decisions. Loving them means allowing them to become who they are, not who we imagined they would be. It also means grieving the dreams we held that may not come true.

When fear takes over, we tend to pressure, shame, or scare our children into belief. However, doing this might secretly send a harmful message: that our religious convictions are more important than they are. That being "right" matters more than building an authentic, loving relationship. Over time, this pressure weakens trust. They may no longer feel safe with us. And when safety is gone, distance increases. The more distance there is, the less influence we have. They become less likely to seek our wisdom, ask honest questions, or value our experience of faith.

The deeper calling of a parent is more challenging and holy. It involves grieving our losses honestly, respecting our children's agency, accepting them as they are, and loving them unconditionally. Our role isn't to convert our children but to reflect God's love in Christ to them.

We can't force faith onto someone else's heart. But we can embody a faith that is patient, humble, and secure enough to allow for doubt. We can build homes where questions are welcomed and where love remains steady regardless of agreement. We can be consistent, compassionate friends when life gets tough, and they begin seeking wisdom beyond themselves.

Ultimately, what shapes our children most deeply is not coercion but love. Not control but character. Not pressure but presence. Our calling is simply to be living, breathing examples of Jesus in the way we love them—especially when they do not choose as we would choose. That kind of love does not guarantee outcomes. But it keeps the relationship intact, so that the way we continue to model the practices in this book can credibly bear witness to the love of God in Jesus.

And we can find comfort in knowing that God understands our children more deeply than we ever could—their questions, doubts, wounds, and longings—and loves them more faithfully than we ever will. God does not abandon them. Through the quiet work of the Holy Spirit and the steady love and faithfulness of God's people, God continues to draw them gently toward grace.

So even if you feel like you've fallen short or if your children or grandchildren have strayed, remember that God is not finished. The seeds you've sown in love are never wasted. The Spirit continues to work in unseen ways, sometimes drawing hearts back in God's timing. Your story, your prayers, and your quiet acts of faithfulness can still bear fruit in unexpected seasons. Take heart: The God who entrusted these children to you is the same God who still holds them.

CONCLUSION

THE WORK OF GRACE AND THE WAY OF LOVE

As I look back over the practices we've explored in this book, I find myself returning to that conversation with the organ salesman who once stopped me in the mall and asked, "Are you saved?"

I said yes—and I meant it. But what I meant was something quite different from what he did. He asked about belief, but I was thinking about the call to discipleship. For Jesus, salvation is not a one-time decision that guarantees our place in heaven but a lifelong journey in which God shapes us into the likeness of Christ as we surrender each day and follow his way of life. Salvation is not only who we are but who we are becoming.

Throughout this book, we've explored what that journey looks like in real life. Christianity is more than believing the right things; it's a daily apprenticeship in love—a living faith cultivated through practice, reflection, and grace. Each chapter has opened a window into this formation, showing how our everyday choices shape our hearts and reveal what we genuinely love.

To be Christian, then, is not merely to *believe* in Jesus but to *practice* his way of life until it becomes our own. Faith without practice becomes weak, hollow, even dangerous. But when we embody faith in daily life, when belief and action move together, it becomes a grace that heals, reconciles, and transforms.

In the Gospels, Jesus never reduces faith to agreeing with ideas about God. Instead, he says, "Follow me." He invites ordinary people to walk with him and learn from him so that they might become a new creation. In the same way, the call of discipleship today is not to prove our theology but to practice the way of Jesus, not to convince others we're right but to live in a way that makes our way of life attractive. It's to embody God's love so authentically that others experience it through us.

The Journey of Transformation

This transformation begins and ends with God's grace. Grace is the heartbeat of the Christian life—the continuous flow of God's love that goes before us, accompanies us, and shapes us into Christ's likeness. It is not something we earn but the presence and power of God at work within us, making possible what we could never achieve on our own. Grace meets us where we are, forgives us when we fail, and patiently shapes us into who God created us to be.

The Christian life is "grace upon grace" (John 1:16). Every step of discipleship is sustained by it. Even when our efforts fall short—and they will—grace carries what we cannot finish. Spiritual growth isn't about self-improvement but about cooperation with divine love.

As we open ourselves to love through these practices, transformation becomes a lifelong rhythm: surrender and renewal, dying and rising, letting go and receiving new life. These practices are not projects but sacred spaces where grace reshapes our hearts.

Over time, the Spirit transforms not only our actions but also our desires. Fear loosens its grip. Pride softens. Resentment gives way to forgiveness. We begin to love what God loves. We see others less as problems and more as beloved children of God. Compassion grows deeper. Hope anchors us. Joy returns.

Spiritual maturity isn't about reaching certainty. It's about developing in love. It's the subtle, Spirit-led formation of a life where belief and practice come together in the likeness of Christ.

The Church as a School of Love

Since transformation begins and ends with grace, it draws us into community where friendship becomes a conduit for God's love. No one follows Jesus alone. The practices that shape us—surrender, forgiveness, empathy, mercy, justice, wrestling with God, and modeling faith—come alive in relationship. Grace flows through us as we live them together.

The church is not a building or organization, but a living community where Christ's love becomes visible. Through worship, prayer, fellowship, and service, the Spirit works within our imperfect relationships, shaping us in love. At its best, the church becomes a school of grace—a place where we learn to forgive, serve, listen, and care. Its witness gains credibility not through power or persuasion, but through the authenticity of its shared life.

This vision extends back to the earliest Christian communities. They dedicated themselves to teaching, fellowship, the breaking of bread, and prayer (Acts 2:42-47). They shared what they had so that no one was in need. They relied on one another, and the Holy Spirit transformed hearts through simple faithfulness. In every era, the church grows not by perfecting its structures but by living out its mission—gathering at the table, praying for the sick, supporting the poor, and listening with compassion.

Of course, the church does not always fulfill this calling. We understand the pain of division and hypocrisy. We've seen how easily fear, pride, and comfort can overshadow humility and love. Yet, even in our shortcomings, grace is abundant. The same Spirit who raised Jesus from the dead continues to mend what we break and calls us back to the way of Christ.

We experience the fullness of salvation not in isolation but in community—sharing meals, carrying burdens, praying through sorrow, and celebrating joy. In these everyday friendships, God shapes and molds us. Our love for God is tested and deepened by the people God places in our lives, especially when loving them is difficult. Here, among imperfect people learning to practice love, grace becomes evident. And as it does, we are quietly formed into the likeness of Christ.

The Cost and the Joy of Discipleship

We need the power of grace that flows through Christian community because nothing worthwhile comes easily. Every practice we've explored stretches us. Love is costly. But take heart; joy awaits on the other side.

When we surrender, we let go of control and find peace. When we forgive, we relinquish our right to get even and experience freedom. When we empathize, we step into another's pain and deepen our love. When we serve, we give what we think we cannot spare and experience God's abundance. When we wrestle with God, we let go of certainty and become present. When we pass faith to the next generation, we relinquish control and learn to trust God with the outcome.

This is the paradox revealed in the cross and resurrection of Jesus: In losing, we gain; in dying, we live; in giving ourselves away, we discover a life that is truly life. The way of the cross becomes the path of joy. These practices might not make life easier, but they deepen it and give it more meaning. They anchor us in a love that overcomes sin, evil, and even death.

Following Jesus always involves risk. It will challenge us and sometimes break our hearts. But even in that breaking, we are not alone. Faith isn't about avoiding pain; it's about learning to find God in the midst of it.

This hope is not naive optimism. It is the steady confidence that God is at work in all things (Romans 8:28) and that nothing can separate us from the love of God in Christ Jesus (Romans 8:38-39). Even when life unravels, grace does not. The God who began a good work in us will be faithful to complete it.

Living the Practices: An Invitation to Ongoing Formation

The practices we've explored are not tasks to check off or disciplines to perfect; they are rhythms of grace that keep us open to transformation. Each one is a way of saying yes to God's love and allowing that love to take deeper root in us.

You can start synchronizing the movement of your life to the rhythm of God's grace by starting simple. Instead of trying to take on every practice at once, remember that spiritual heroics usually end in disappointment. The goal isn't to master everything but to take one faithful step at a time. Ask God to show you which practice will be most helpful for dealing with challenges that will come today. Then start there and start small. Trust that grace meets you in simple beginnings and that, over time, those small steps will lead to deep and lasting change.

This might mean beginning each morning with a simple prayer of surrender: "God, I relinquish control and place my life in your hands. Show me your will and give me the power to carry it out." Or it may look like meditating on a short passage of Scripture and listening for God's still, small voice. If you wrestle with busyness, pause during the day to notice God's presence—in a conversation, in the beauty of creation, or in a quiet act of kindness that passes between strangers. When resentment surfaces, choose forgiveness. When you encounter someone in pain, practice empathy. When you notice a need and can help in some small way, respond with mercy and justice. When life brings questions you cannot answer, keep wrestling with God, trusting that blessing often comes through struggle. As you walk alongside younger believers, model and teach these practices with patience and grace as they learn them in their own way.

These small acts, repeated over time, become holy habits that train us in love and deeply shape who we become. They turn belief into practice, practice into character, and character into witness.

Through these ordinary disciplines, God's extraordinary grace transforms us from the inside out.

There will be times when you feel like you're failing more than succeeding. Faith will sometimes feel strong and clear, and at other times frail and uncertain. Don't be discouraged; this is normal. Formation is never finished, and we often grow most through adversity. So, when you struggle to hold onto God, trust that God will never let go of you. Give yourself grace. The goal is not perfection but progress through participation: learning to live each day in sync with the rhythm of Christ's transforming love.

The beauty of these practices is that they ripple outward, becoming a witness to the love of God in the world. As we live them, we embody the gospel in the small, faithful acts of everyday discipleship. Children learn faith by seeing faith in action. Neighbors glimpse grace through everyday acts of kindness. Strangers experience compassion that rekindles hope. When Christians live this way, the good news becomes visible, not as a set of ideas to defend but as a life shaped by love.

This is how the church renews its witness in a divided world: through surrendered hearts, acts of mercy, and moments of empathy that reveal the character of Christ. In a culture weary of words and suspicious of institutions, we don't persuade people with arguments about our beliefs but by living according to the law of love. Every time Christians forgive one another, care for the vulnerable, listen across differences, or work for justice, we create a signpost pointing to Jesus.

These practices don't just show what we believe; they make what we believe more believable. They reveal that grace is more than a religious talking point; it is the divine power that heals what is broken and reconciles what is torn apart. When faith takes visible shape in love, it bridges the gap between what the world suspects about the church and what God still knows it can become.

When the church embodies this kind of love, its testimony gains credibility, not because we have solved every problem or arrived at absolute truth, but because grace itself is trustworthy. God's love shines through imperfect people who keep showing up, keep serving, and keep believing that Jesus's love still has the power to heal the world.

The Broader Vision: Participating in God's Renewal

As we engage in the practices of this book—often imperfectly and with faltering steps—it's important to remember that we're participating in something far greater than our own spiritual growth. Every act of faithful love joins God's magnificent work of renewing all things. This is why Jesus taught us to pray,

> *May your kingdom come.*
> *May your will be done,*
> *on earth as it is in heaven*
> *(Matthew 6:10 NRSVue)*

Each time we forgive, we interrupt cycles of resentment and violence and point toward God's dream of a world made whole in peace. Each time we act with empathy, we bridge divides and bear witness to the reconciling power of love. Each time we stand for justice, we proclaim the coming kingdom already breaking into our present reality in the power of the Holy Spirit.

The early church described this mystery as *theosis*—the grace-filled process by which God transforms us to share in the divine life and reflect the character of divine love. This transformation does not make us divine, but points to how God through Christ in the power of the Holy Spirit, makes us "participants of the divine nature" (2 Peter 1:4 NRSVue). Rather than losing our humanity, we find it restored, fully alive and reflecting more clearly the image of Jesus. This means that when we follow Jesus, even our smallest actions matter, because God uses them to draw creation toward its fulfillment in love.

The practices we've explored in this book—surrender, forgiveness, empathy, mercy, justice, wrestling with God, and modeling faith—are the ways God draws us into the current of divine love that flows through all creation. As we are shaped by that love, we become conduits of grace for the healing of the world. So to live as a Christian is not simply to seek our own happiness, but to take part in God's redemption of all things.

This broad vision keeps our practices from shrinking into mere self-improvement, reminding us that they are not strategies for personal success but means of grace by which God's love becomes visible in the world.

What Christians Do—and Who They Become

In the end, we cannot separate what we as Christians do from who we are becoming. Practice and identity are two sides of the same mystery. Each time we forgive, show empathy, serve others, wrestle with God, or bear witness to Christ, we take part in the ongoing work of the Spirit, who is reshaping humanity into the image of Jesus and making all things new.

To say "This is what Christians do" is not to boast of our goodness but to confess our utter dependence on God's grace. Every act of love, every step of faithfulness, is God's work in us and through us. And yet, our transformation also requires our grace-enabled willingness to follow Jesus by imitating his way of life. God will not force us to change. Love always invites; it never coerces. The Spirit waits for our yes. But when we do respond, however imperfectly, we join the great movement of redemption that began before us and will continue long after us.

The practices explored in this book are not isolated notes but part of a greater melody of grace. Together they create a harmony that reveals the beauty of life in Christ—humble, compassionate, courageous, and real. They remind us that the Christian life is not a strenuous climb toward perfection but a dance to the rhythm of love, where we keep learning together what it means to trust, to serve, to forgive, to heal, and to hope.

If there is a single thread running through *What Christians Do*, it is this: Love is the beginning, the middle, and the end of the Christian life, as Jesus teaches us in the Greatest Commandment (Mark 12:29-31). Love is what calls us into being, what sustains us through life, and what will one day make all things new. And that love is not abstract. It becomes real and tangible whenever we practice the way of Jesus.

So let us go and live this faith in the world.

Let us be people who surrender daily to God's grace.

Let us forgive as we have been forgiven.

Let us practice empathy that connects us to the perspective and pain of others.

Let us serve with mercy and seek justice for the least of these.

Let us wrestle faithfully with God until blessing emerges from the struggle.

Let us share faith with humility, honesty, and joy.

And through it all, let us remember that God is transforming us into the likeness of Christ.

In the end, this is what Christians do.

So when someone asks "Are you saved?" let us answer: *Yes! I am saved,* ***and*** *I am being saved—for love, for grace, and for the sake of the world.* And may the shape of our lives bear faithful witness to this truth.

NOTES

Chapter 1

1 John Wesley, "The Almost Christian" (1741), in *John Wesley's Sermons: An Anthology*, ed. Albert C. Outler and Richard P. Heitzenrater (Abingdon Press, 1991).

2 Dietrich Bonhoeffer, *The Cost of Discipleship* (Touchstone, 1995), 44–45.

Chapter 2

1 My understanding of forgiveness has been deeply shaped by the writings of Miroslav Volf, especially his book *Free of Charge: Giving and Forgiving in a Culture Stripped of Grace* (Zondervan, 2005).

Chapter 5

1 Peter Enns, *The Sin of Certainty: Why God Desires Our Trust More Than Our "Correct" Beliefs* (HarperOne, 2016).

Chapter 6

1 "The Baptismal Covenant II," *The United Methodist Book of Worship* (The United Methodist Book of Worship, 1992).

2 Christian Smith and Melinda Lundquist Denton, *Soul Searching: The Religious and Spiritual Lives of American Teenagers* (Oxford University Press, 2005).